MOUTHSOUNDS

How to whistle, pop, click, and honk your way to social success

MOUTHSOUNDS

How to whistle, pop, click, and honk your way to social success

FREDERICK R. NEWMAN

ILLUSTRATED BY MARTY NORMAN
PHOTOGRAPHS BY JERRY DARVIN

WORKMAN PUBLISHING, NEW YORK

This book is dedicated to the little guys—the class clowns and the office cutups. Those unsung heroes who, in addition to shooting paper clips and photocopying their faces, rescue us from what would otherwise be lackluster afternoons.

Copyright © 1980 by Frederick R. Newman

Library of Congress Cataloging in Publication Data

Newman, Frederick R.
Mouthsounds.

1. Amusements. 2. Mouth—Sounds. I. Title.
GV1201.N44   790.1   80-51613
ISBN 0-89480-128-7

Jacket design: Paul Hanson
Jacket photograph: Jerry Darvin

Workman Publishing
1 West 39 Street
New York, New York 10018

Manufactured in the
United States of America
10   9   8   7   6   5   4   3   2   1

ACKNOWLEDGMENTS

I would like to thank those people who helped so much in advising, designing, and generally guiding this book to reality:

Jan Borene, Nancy Boykin, Ann Brody, Joan Braucher, Jerri Buckley, Jerry Darvin, Donna Gould, Sweet Victoria Hamilton, Paul Hanson, Jim Harrison, Alison Karlsson, Sally Kovalchick, Cacky Daniel McKenzie, Marty Norman, Wendy Palitz, Kathryn Placzek, Christopher Power, Jennifer Rogers, Helene Siegel, Marjorie Singer, Bert Snyder, Jack Eric Williams, Peter Workman.

My special thanks to those individuals who put their upwardly mobile careers on the line by posing for photographs:

Adam Aaron, Bruce Batkin, Chuck Berman, Lisa Birnbach, Peter Bonventre, Jan Borene, John Boyd, Ann Brody, Jerri Buckley, Cynthia Busbee, Alison Clarkson, Esther Cohen, Jerry Darvin, Leon Darvin, Richard Edelman, Billy German, Donna Gould, Barbara Grecki, Victoria Hamilton, Paul Hanson, Jim Harrison, Henry Hirsch, Anne-Marie Huber, Sallie Jackson, Carrie Jones, Karen Juliana, Ellen Kavan, Sally Kovalchick, Paul Kowal, Charles Kreloff, Julie Lazar, Lenny Levine, John Levy, Barbara Lewis, Ruth McKown, Marty Norman, Carmille Norman, Mark O'Donnell, Steven O'Donnell, David Olsen, Christopher Power, Bill Rayman, Rob Rosecrans, Jennifer Rogers, George Rohr, Joe Romano, Sarah Skolnik, Stu Slater, Bert Snyder, Lisa Tumbleson, Darrell Vange, Ina Weisser, Peter Williams, David Winn, Tyrone Wyatt, Carmile Zaino.

And finally, my love, thanks, and gratitude to my mother and father in Georgia who have shaken their heads on more than one occasion and wondered: "Where did we go wrong?"

CONTENTS

*THE
SLAP
POP*

*THE
FALSETTO*

*THE
LANDING*

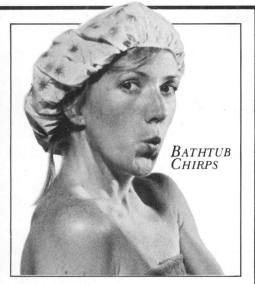

Bathtub Chirps

Herd of Elephants

CHAPTER FIVE

CHAPTER SIX

CHAPTER SEVEN

The Takeoff

The Telephone Dial

Robot Whirrs

The Classic Raspberry

CHAPTER EIGHT

RUDE NOISES

Civilizations come and go. The swish of arrows is stilled by the crack of rifles. Gallops give way to engine whirrs; the clink of chalices becomes the crunch of Dixie cups. Through sounds we come to know society.

Sounds provide the cues by which we pace our lives. We begin the day with the zing of the alarm clock. The creak of the opening door tells us the bathroom is free. The teakettle whistles. The phone rings. The dog barks as the newspaper boy slings the daily newspaper on the front porch.

The subtleties of sounds provide clues, communicate, and connect.

But so many sounds spew forth from the complexities of this modern age that we have almost become numbed. We can live a lifetime without once pausing to appreciate the croak of a frog, the clang of a bell, or the crackle of cellophane.

Mouthsounds is a book as much about listening as it is about imitating sounds. To imitate, we must first cultivate our ability to listen.

No instrument ever devised has the range and ability to

manipulate sounds as does the human voice. We talk, yell, whisper, laugh, and sing with natural ease.

By attempting to imitate sounds around us, we extend our vocabulary into new realms of acoustic color. We can better communicate and entertain, astound and amuse. We are able to garnish a story or a conversation with sound effects sure to widen eyes and raise eyebrows.

Mouthsounds speaks to the whistles, pops, clicks, and honks that lie within each of us.

AN EXCURSION INTO THE MOUTH

THE RAND McNALLY OF THE ORAL CAVITY

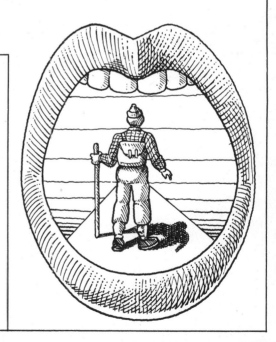

The human voice mechanism is an amazing thoroughfare. From the back roads of the lungs, air passes over the vocal folds, generating sound vibrations. These vibrations travel up the four-lane highway of the throat into the echoing valleys of the mouth and nose, where the scenery adds color, variety, and richness to the sound. The sound vibrations then speed past the lips, out of the mouth, and into the ears of listeners. It is a quick trip, taking only fractions of a second to accomplish, but it is one of our most reliable, yet complex, routes for sending messages to others.

The vocal mechanism is really an instrument that involves the coordinated use of several separate structures of the body: the lungs, which act as the power source; the vocal folds, which generate the sound vibrations; and the throat, nose, and mouth, which act as resonators and amplifiers of the sound.

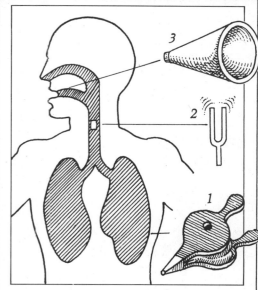

1. The lungs act as a pair of bellows, providing power for the voice

2. The larynx or voice box sets up voice vibrations, much like a tuning fork

3. The mouth and pharynx act as an amplifying megaphone for sound

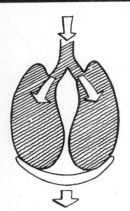

THE INHALE

Diaphragm is contracted and lowered, enlarging the chest cavity, drawing in air.

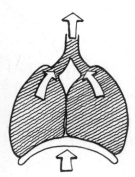

THE EXHALE

Diaphragm is relaxed, shrinking the chest cavity, pressing out air from our lungs.

The Lungs. The lungs are like a pair of plastic bags suspended in the chest cavity. They have no ability to move or inflate themselves, but, as we breathe, they are filled with air by the use of chest muscles, in particular the diaphragm. The lungs provide the air pressure necessary to make the vocal folds vibrate.

The Diaphragm. The diaphragm is the single most important muscle in breathing. It is a powerful sheet of muscular tissue that separates the chest cavity from the abdominal cavity. Inhalation takes place as we contract and lower the diaphragm, enlarging the chest cavity, thereby pulling air into our lungs. To exhale, we simply relax the diaphragm, the chest cavity shrinks, and presses out air from our lungs. As we speak loudly or sing, we use other abdominal and chest muscles to squeeze the chest cavity, forcing more rapid exhalation of air.

The Larynx. The larynx, or what vocal dunces call the "voice box," is the tube-shaped mechanism in the throat that houses and protects the vocal folds. It consists of many delicate muscles and nine cartilages, the most prominent of which forms the hard lump in the throat we call the Adam's apple. Air exhaled from the lungs passes through the larynx between the vocal folds and makes them vibrate.

The Vocal Folds. Vocal folds should not be called "vocal cords," for they are not cordlike at all, but actually two infoldings of the mucous membrane that lines the larynx. They are connected across the windpipe or trachea in an elastic, V-shaped configuration. The two vocal folds are fixed together at the front of the throat, with the other end of each fold connected separately to two mobile cartilages at the back of the throat. The cartilages are moved by muscles, pulling the vocal folds together, allowing them to vibrate in the stream of air from the lungs.

The vocal folds function very much like the pinched neck of an inflated balloon that any skillful party goer worth his salt can stretch

THE SEXY VOICE

The soft, low purr of female voices used by Madison Avenue to hawk anything from automobiles to panty hose is no accidental advertising ploy. The sexiness of that husky whisper rests squarely in biology. During sexual excitement and lovemaking, the mucous membrane of the larynx undergoes physical changes that cause the voice, particularly the female voice, to become lower and huskier. The soft, low coos of singers and film stars trace back to imitations of this sexual voice. Admired by men and simulated by women, this voice has nearly universal sex appeal.

CUTAWAY VIEW OF THE VOCAL FOLDS

Vocal folds relaxed at sides of windpipe for normal breathing

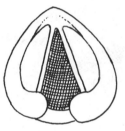

Vocal folds drawn in slightly for a soft whisper

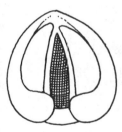

Vocal folds drawn closer together for a loud "stage" whisper

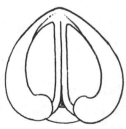

Vocal folds pulled completely together for full vibration or normal speech

and contort to produce a rubbery squeal. The pinched folds of the balloon neck vibrate as air from the balloon passes between them producing the familiar, albeit, obnoxious, whine. For a whisper, we pull the folds only slightly together, but for full speech or singing, the folds are drawn in completely.

Using a complex array of muscles in and around the larynx, we change the pitch of our vocal sounds. To sing the familiar "do, re, mi" musical scale, various muscles stretch our vocal folds, making them thinner. The thinner the vocal folds the faster the vibrations and the higher the pitch of the tone—again like stretching the neck of a party balloon raises the pitch of the squeal.

The False Vocal Folds. Directly above the vocal folds are two "false vocal folds." The false folds are not used for vocalization but, like the vocal folds, are used to help protect the lungs from inhaling debris. When the false folds are tightly drawn together, they help us to hold our breath.

Not a large deal you might think, but our lungs could collapse were it not for the fact that we involuntarily hold our breath when we exert ourselves physically. In activities ranging from lifting furniture to swinging a bat, we automatically hold our breath, protecting our lungs from collapse. (We should be thankful that we manage to keep on good terms with these important little flaps of mucous membrane.)

BREATHING

It should come as no surprise that breathing is a fairly basic fact of life. Fortunately, breathing is automatic. We do not have to think about it. Otherwise we would have to constantly leave notes to ourselves reminding us to inhale.

But, many people breathe incorrectly. We often breathe only with our upper chest by raising and lowering the rib cage. This type of breathing is very shallow and very energy consuming.

Correct breathing is important for good health and good articulation. It involves breathing "from the stomach," or, more correctly, with the diaphragm. When we sleep, the body naturally breathes this way to conserve energy.

Lie down on the floor. Place your hand on your stomach and feel your stomach rise and fall quite naturally as you breathe from your diaphragm. Now sit up straight and continue breathing slowly from your stomach. This is how you should always breathe.

Good posture and correct breathing actually improve your projection and ability to speak by helping to maintain proper breath control. Because many of the sounds included in this book require large amounts of air, proper breathing is especially important.

The Pharynx, Mouth, and Nose.
Once a vocal tone is generated by the larynx, it must be strengthened and enhanced by resonation within the pharynx, mouth, and nasal passages, just as guitars, violins, and other stringed instruments must have a body to add to and amplify their fundamental musical tones. The pharynx is the elastic chamber extending up from the larynx to the back of the mouth. The roof of the pharynx is the soft palate or velum which acts as the door to the nasal cavities. (No doubt you have noticed the little punching bag hanging from the soft palate in the back of your mouth. This is the uvula which, although it serves no real purpose, is interesting to look at in the mirror.) When the velum is raised it closes off the nasal cavities, thereby cutting off nasal resonance, changing the sound of the tone.

At the base of the tongue, just at the top of the windpipe, is the epiglottis. This flap of tissue helps prevent food from entering the larynx. In reality, however, the epiglottis is merely a vestigial remnant of a larger cartilage flap once used to seal off the mouth while eating. In that way, the defensive sense of smell would not be interfered with during eating.

As the pharynx, mouth, and nose cavities vibrate with vocal tones, sound complexity increases giving the human voice its richness and versatility. Relaxing the walls of the pharynx dampens the higher frequencies of the voice and accen-

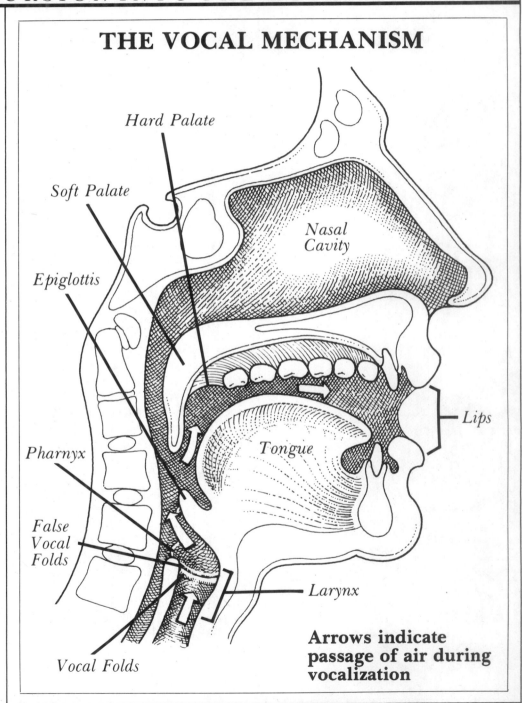

THE VOCAL MECHANISM

Hard Palate

Soft Palate

Epiglottis

Nasal Cavity

Lips

Pharnyx

Tongue

False Vocal Folds

Larynx

Vocal Folds

Arrows indicate passage of air during vocalization

tuates the lower frequencies, thus producing a more mellow voice. Hard or taut muscular walls act more like reflectors, producing harsher tones.

Speech is formed as the pharynx and mouth change size and shape to produce vowel sounds, while the tongue and lips clip tones into consonants. When this spectrum of resonance is combined with the range and flexibility of the vocal folds themselves, we have a truly amazing instrument.

The Brain and its Control of the Voice. Exactly how the brain controls the voice is not completely understood. We do know that, unlike "lower" animals, humans have several centers in the dominant brain hemisphere that aid in vocalization. Usually, at least for right-handed people, these centers are located on the left side of the brain near the temple in a part of the brain known as Broca's area. It controls the muscles of the mouth and throat and coordinates other complex bodily movements—such as breathing—that are so necessary for speech and singing.

A second center, Wernike's area—just behind Broca's area—is responsible for the structure and sense of our language. As we speak, Wernike's area takes auditory information from our ears as feedback, and informs the speaker about such qualities as pitch, volume, and inflection of the voice.

When we want to say something like "Hold the mustard," Wernike's area organizes words into a basic grammatical form and then sends signals to Broca's area to coordinate breathing, vocal folds, mouth, and lips so that a quick "Hold the mustard" issues forth just in time.

It is interesting that singing, as opposed to speech, involves separate neural mechanisms that are located deep within primitive areas of the brain dealing with emotional activity. Often when a stroke causes such brain damage that a person cannot speak, the person is still able to sing with fine articulation, and even severe stutterers can sometimes sing without any problems.

The complexity of speaking and singing require a great deal of brain space; so much so, that over Broca's and Wernike's areas are slight lumps, making the left side of the brain larger than the right.

HEARING

The ear, like the voice, is an astounding instrument. The importance of hearing in providing auditory feedback cannot be overstated. We learn to speak and sing by imitation. Only by listening closely to our attempts at vocalization do we come to approximate sounds and control the range of our voices.

The human ear responds to sounds that are really minute changes in air pressure repeated in rapid succession. The ear, in fact, is so sensitive to waves of sound vibrations that changes in atmospheric pressure of one part in ten billion, if repeated about 3,500 times a second, send audible signals to the brain. In receiving such a sound, the eardrum moves less than one-tenth the diameter of the smallest atom. If our ears were more sensitive, we would probably be able to hear the actual motion of air molecules as they vibrate with heat energy.

Humans can distinguish sound vibrations ranging from a low of about 16 vibrations per second to a high of about 20,000 per second, with heightened sensitivity to those sounds falling within the range of 1,000 to 4,000 vibrations per second.

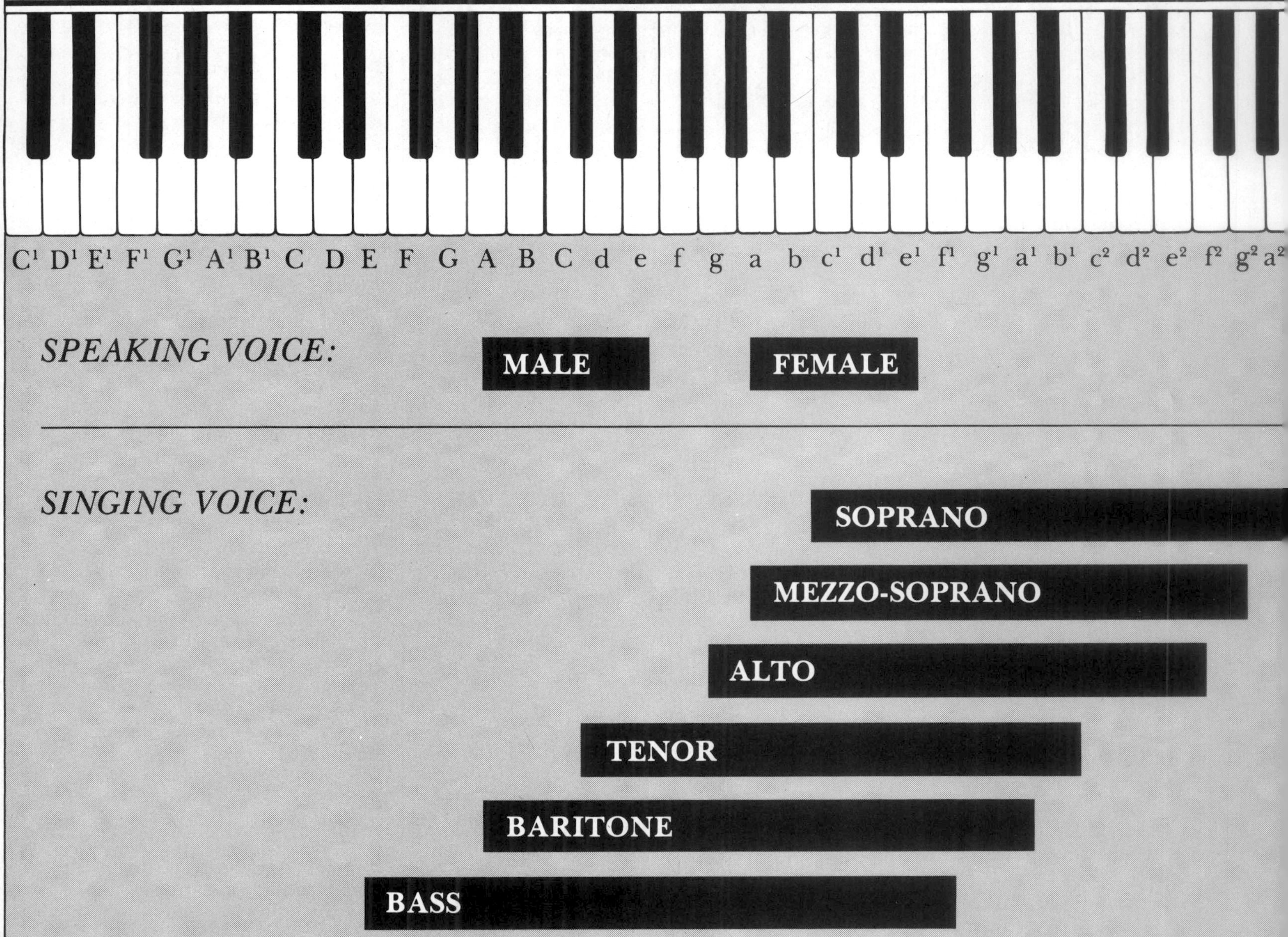

C¹ D¹ E¹ F¹ G¹ A¹ B¹ C D E F G A B C d e f g a b c¹ d¹ e¹ f¹ g¹ a¹ b¹ c² d² e² f² g² a²

SPEAKING VOICE:

MALE   **FEMALE**

SINGING VOICE:

SOPRANO

MEZZO-SOPRANO

ALTO

TENOR

BARITONE

BASS

THE RANGE OF THE HUMAN VOICE

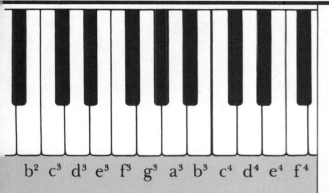

b² c³ d³ e³ f³ g³ a³ b³ c⁴ d⁴ e⁴ f⁴

WHISTLE REGISTER

Vocal Range. Vocal pitch is determined by the speed with which the vocal folds vibrate to produce the tone of the voice. Pitch is measured in vibrations or cycles per second (or "Hertz," for electronic buffs.)

The range of the voice is dependent upon the size of larynx as related to sex, age, and body type, while the exact pitch within a given range is dictated by such variables as tension of the vocal folds and air pressure.

The Art of Singing. Singing requires all the skills that speaking does, but demands increased breath capacity and control over longer phrases. Speech uses gliding voice inflections with sudden changes in volume and pitch to give meaning to syllables. Usually the pitch will slide up and down a limited scale of tones—about one octave, three or four notes above and below a middle note.

Singing differs from speaking in that a rhythmical melody is usually followed over precise musical intervals. Pitch changes in singing over one-and-a-half octaves in untrained voices and three or more octaves in trained voices. Unlike speech, singing requires the development of a musical "ear" to hear notes, and the development of absolute control over vocal musculature is necessary to prevent the voice from sliding off key—with the consequence that people throw things at you.

Types of Voices. The adult voice is classified according to its range. Of course, each voice has its own peculiarities but, in general, male voices are roughly divided into bass, baritone, and tenor voices, while female voices are divided into contralto, mezzo-soprano, and soprano. The chart outlines these categories and the approximate range of each.

THE HIGHEST AND LOWEST NOTES

The lowest note written for vocal performance is a low "D" (73 cycles per second) at the end of Osmin's aria in Mozart's opera *The Abduction from the Seraglio*. The highest note is a high F, almost 1,400 cycles per second, sung by the Queen of the Night in *The Magic Flute*.

THE COUGH

Without the use of our false vocal cords and our ability to coordinate a cough, we would be unable to clear our lungs of unpleasant things such as excess mucus or Pepsi that has "gone down the wrong way."

During a cough, we quickly inhale air as the diaphragm descends forcefully. The vocal folds and false vocal folds close tightly. As we tense our abdominal muscles, air pressure builds in our lungs to the point that the folds are suddenly exploded apart, and the Pepsi, Fritos, and bean dip are expelled.

Coughs are most often a spontaneous bodily reaction to the tickle of unwanted matter in the lungs; but occasionally we can use the cough to social advantage. A fained coughing attack allows you an acceptable quick exit from such tedious situations as accounting lectures, droning church sermons, and amateur productions of Hamlet.

The life-saving aspects of the cough cannot be overestimated. Indeed, the cough is nothing to be sneezed at.

Registers. The term "vocal register" is not a scientific term at all, but one that has been used over centuries to describe the location of vibrating sensations of certain vocal tones. There are three basic registers: the chest voice, mid-voice, and head voice, reflecting the fact that low notes are felt primarily in the chest, while high notes are felt in the head.

The chest and head voices may be more scientifically called the "thick" and "thin" voices, because a cross section of the vibrating vocal folds shows that the lowest tunes are produced by a marked thickening of the vocal folds, which forms a richer tone, full of resonant chest vibrations. The high notes of the head voice are produced by tensing and thinning the vocal folds to create a less "rounded" sound that resonates in the upper throat, mouth, and nose.

Still another register is used by the highest of sopranos to produce extremely high notes. It is called the "whistle register," and is called so because the vocal folds are tensed to a razor-sharp edge, allowing a small, elliptical hole to form between them. The vocal folds do not even vibrate. The singer literally whistles through this small hole.

SCHEMATIC CROSS SECTION OF VOCAL FOLDS

Vocal folds thick for the lower, chest or "thick" register

Vocal folds thinned somewhat for mid-voice register

Vocal folds very thin for the higher, head or "thin" register

THE CASTRATI: THE FORERUNNERS OF THE BEE GEES

Few realize that the high-voiced harmonies of the Bee Gees date back nearly 2,000 years to the Roman era. To achieve such falsetto, the Romans castrated gifted young male singers. As one can imagine, this put a stop to the natural maturation of their voices, producing male singers with high, soprano voices, known as *soprani falsetti*. These singers exhibited amazing range and power and enjoyed very privileged positions among the Roman elite for many years, but quickly disappeared with the crumble of the Roman Empire.

In the early sixteenth century, the Renaissance witnessed a rekindling of interest in Greek and Roman culture. Vocal music in the Western church was growing much more complex and talented choirboys were quite scarce. Once again, innocent youths were tapped for *soprani falsetti*, or "castrati," as they were called in the Middle Ages. By the mid-sixteenth century, the castrati had become an integral part of religious celebrations in Spain, and in 1562, Father Soto, a well-known Spanish castrato, drew official church recognition of the castrati upon his entering the choir of the Sistine Chapel.

With their astounding vocal abilities, the castrati soon came to dominate the art of singing. For almost two hundred years, it was a virtual tradition among musical families to have a member of the family in a leading church choir, and castration was frequently resorted to in order to uphold this tradition.

By the end of the nineteenth century, castration for the sake of music was looked upon as a bit extreme, and the castrati were replaced by young male singers and falsettists. The last castrato, Alessandro Moreschi, died in 1922.

Interest in the male falsetto voice waned during the first half of the twentieth century, and use of falsetto singing was limited to English church choirs, novelty vaudeville acts, and Negro minstrel shows.

In the late 1940s, however, a revival of falsetto occurred among Black spiritual song groups. These groups influenced the high harmonies of popular a cappella singing in the 1950s. In the 1960s, groups such as the Four Seasons and the Beach Boys made tremendously successful use of falsetto harmonies.

At the same time, falsetto witnessed a revival in "legitimate" music. The role of Oberon in Benjamin Britten's musical *A Midsummer Night's Dream* was sung in falsetto.

The long, if somewhat checkered, history of high-voiced male singing has most recently culminated in the disco reincarnation of the Bee Gees. Their tight, falsetto harmonies combined with the cadencelike pounding of disco to create a distinctively new—and distinctly lucrative—sound in America.

THE ANTHROPOLOGICAL ORIGINS OF SPEECH

Just when and why man developed the distinctively human characteristic of speech continues to be wrapped in speculation. It is generally thought, however, that in the three billion years of evolutionary cakewalk, from primordial sludge to Warren Beatty, man's capacity to speak came very late.

Sometime around two million years B.C., man's ancestor the Australopithecus turned from a comfortable vegetarian diet to a menu that included meat—possibly as a result of climactic changes. One theory suggests that meat, as a more concentrated protein source, effectively cut by two-thirds the time spent gathering berries and various fruits, and with more free time, man was able to extend himself in creative and social directions. An increasingly complex hunting and food-gathering society resulted, with increased demands for communication.

Imagine, for example, an unarmed, naked man trying to down a rampaging woolly mammoth. Without the development of weapons—and language to coordinate other naked men—the woolly mammoth would have had a field day. (In the long process of language development, no doubt, a lot of confused, naked men were flattened.)

During this time, the brain was developing rapidly. With the coming of *Homo erectus* around one million B.C., man walked erect, thereby freeing his hands for experimentation and tool formation. Manual dexterity grew as the brain developed refinements and areas of specialization. The result was a preference for either left- or right-hand use and the distinctively human characteristic of dominance of one brain hemisphere over the other. By this specialization, brain capacity was increased tremendously, and the areas of speech control became located in a dominant side of the brain, usually the left side for right-handed people.

The vocal mechanism, too, was evolving rapidly. Unlike other animals, the great dexterity of man's hands freed his oral cavity from the process of direct food-gathering, allowing the development of vocal articulation. The vocal folds, originally protective flaps for the windpipe, began to be used to produce primitive sounds for communication. The larynx, containing the vocal folds, descended, and the upper throat—the pharynx—became wider, thus allowing more resonant vocal possibilities and the capacity for producing vowel sounds.

All these various developments occurred quite quickly in terms of evolution, each development being intimately linked to others. Man's manual experimentation contributed to his brain development, which, in turn, aided speech development. At the same time, the invention of spoken words meant an imposition

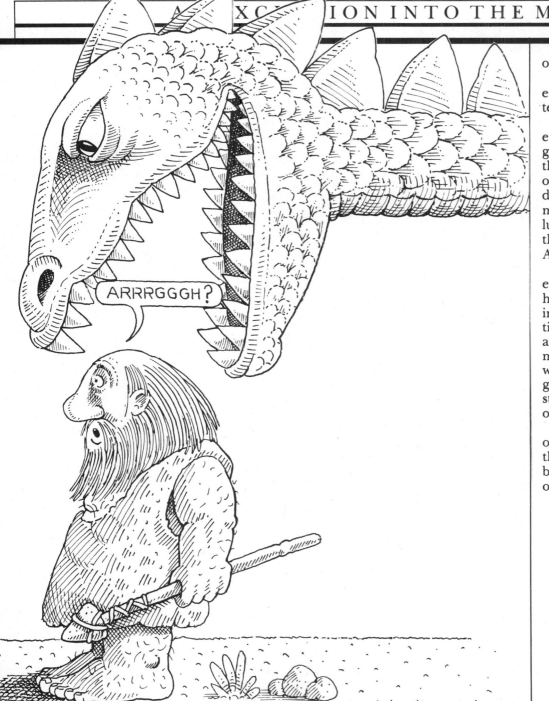

ARRRGGGH?

of mental order on the world.

This allowed man to *think* more effectively, thus enhancing his intellectual facilities.

Recent theories suggest that the evolution of human speech made great leaps forward about seventy thousand years ago, during the era of the fourth Ice Age. For Neanderthal man, with a brain the size of modern man, speech became absolutely necessary for survival under the cataclysmic challenges of the Ice Age.

From that point on, the social evolution of man exploded. The human population began increasing, spurred by the cultural sophistication that arose from language and speech development. Primitive man populated the world. Writing was invented. Three thousand languages developed. And modern man stepped forth to claim dominance over the world.

The long and glorious process of elbowing our way to the front of the animal kingdom has certainly been spurred by the development of the human voice.

THE PRINCIPLES OF MOUTHSOUNDS

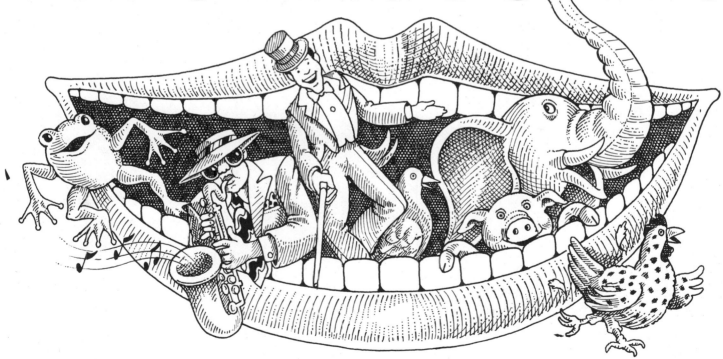

ON BECOMING A MASTER

ONE

The best introduction to the world of mouth sounds is, first of all, to listen to the mouth sounds record. Through the miracle of modern vinyl, the record will enable you to hear each of the sounds described in the book and give you an idea of the range of vocal possibilities. All the sounds on the record, including background music, are vocally produced.

TWO

It is highly recommended that you begin by reading the first two chapters, for they provide a basic understanding of the voice mechanism and vocal principles, as well as useful fodder for the casual conversation.

THREE

Read the chapters, either in a secluded spot or in the company of understanding friends. Always try the sounds *out loud*, using the mouth sounds record as a guide. The record gives you a sample of each sound. Following the text directions and diagrams provided, you should then try to approximate the sound, listening carefully to your own voice. As any winning football coach would say, practice, of course, is essential.

FOUR

After you have mastered a few sounds, work up the nerve to try out a few during, say, a lull in conversation over dinner or cocktails. You will be surprised how the sounds can give just that lighter touch to a heavy intellectual discussion.

FIVE

Use the book and record as party entertainment. It is great fun to hear others attempt the sounds, and, what's more, you increase your self-esteem by making your friends look foolish.

SIX

Begin listening to sounds around you, drawing them into your new and rapidly expanding repertory. With each new sound you master, you develop increased vocal control and flexibility, thereby increasing your ability to master even more sounds.

Do not be discouraged if you cannot master sounds immediately. Like dieting or dancing, nothing happens to your pounds or pirouettes until you allow sufficient time and practice. No less than dance, oral acrobatics require the delicate orchestration of muscles—almost sixty muscles, in fact, are required just to sing the notes "do, re, mi." No less than dieting, sheer willpower and time are essential.

So persevere. With a little bit of effort on your part, you will soon be able to dazzle, delight, and yes, even stupefy your fellow man.

THE FALSETTO

The true falsetto or "false soprano" voice is the high-pitched, slightly breathy voice that can be effected by most people.

Falsetto is produced by allowing only part of the vocal folds to vibrate. In male falsetto, the short vibrating portion of the vocal folds closely approximates the length of the female vocal folds, thus making the high falsetto of a male sound much like a female voice. With only the front portion of the folds drawn together to vibrate, the voice is made slightly breathy as air passes through the space between the nonvibrating portion of the vocal folds.

INSTRUCTIONS

You can probably produce a falsetto voice easily, but if you cannot, do the following: In a normal tone, let your voice glide upward from low notes to high notes, without increasing the loudness as you increase the pitch. At some point for males, and most females, your voice will "break" as it gets higher. You will hear a sudden distinct change in the quality of your voice as the falsetto shortening of the vocal fold vibration occurs. (This break, by the way, is the basic principle of yodeling.) You should practice talking and singing with the falsetto voice. Many of the sounds in *Mouthsounds* will require the use of this voice in males or a similar high-pitched voice in females.

For falsetto, only part of the vocal folds vibrate

THE FALSETTO

THE PLOIT

RESONANCE

Besides the vocal folds, the single most important tool in your noisemaking tool chest is resonance. When you whistle, click, or pop, you do not use your vocal folds at all. It is possible to use your lips or tongue or perhaps your hand to cause vibrations that are then molded into a sound by the shape of your mouth and throat.

The Ploit, a hollow thump of a sound, illustrates this basic principle of resonance.

INSTRUCTIONS

1. Close off the back of your opened mouth by breathing normally through your nose.

2. Draw your tongue to the back of your mouth. Shape your mouth and lips as if you were going to sing a very low "o."

3. With your finger, tap or thump the hollow of your cheek like a drum.

By raising your tongue and the bottom of your mouth together, you can raise and lower the pitch of your Ploit to produce musical tones. Practice until you can lilt

your way through such favorites as "Yankee Doodle" or "Home on the Range." Mastering the Ploit principle will serve you well, for it forms the base of many mouth sounds.

Back of tongue arched to close off mouth

THE PLOIT

THE PALATE GRIND

The Palate Grind is a basic mouth sound technique that forms the foundation of such diverse sounds as hand saws, trains, and drum rolls. It is the sound many children use to imitate guns and explosions.

Blow out with back of tongue arched up to roof of mouth

INSTRUCTIONS

1. Arch the back of your tongue upward to touch far back on the rear ceiling of your mouth, in the area known as the soft palate (page 18).

2. Blow out air so that the back of your tongue and the soft palate vibrate with a gravelly, grinding sound. (Record)

This is the Palate Grind that will be used to make various mouth sounds in the book. By moving the arched tongue to different points on the soft palate and varying the air pressure, you can produce different tones.

THE PALATE GRIND

POP, CLICKS, HORNS & HONKS

Pops, clicks, snaps, bangs, horns, and honks make our mechanized world go around. Clicks, snaps, and bangs are the byproducts of bridled energy, harnessed by man to build, move, take apart things and put them together. Horns and honks, on the other hand, are the signals of modern society, meant to prod, poke, provoke, and cajole us into action. This chapter deals with some of the technological sounds that continually zip through our lives.

THE CHAMPAGNE POP

POPS

Pops come in many shapes and sizes. Some are so faint only mothers can hear them. Others are deafening. Machines pop, bottles pop, people pop—even animals pop (think of the weasel). Pops can be playful, and pops can be harmful to your health.

But in every case, a pop is a clear signal something is happening—or just about to.

The Champagne Pop is the classic mouth sound. Historically, it has been used by enterprising adolescents to disrupt more study halls than, perhaps, any other single sound—with the possible exception of the Bronx Cheer.

INSTRUCTIONS

1. Insert one index finger into your mouth. The palm of your hand should face away from you. (If at this point you taste something funny, make a mental note to wash your hands.)

2. Seal your lips around the first and second knuckle of your finger. Puff out your cheeks with as much air as possible.

3. Quickly pry your finger out of your mouth so that the tip of the finger snaps the corner of the mouth. *Pop!* (Record).

It may take a bit of practice, but you will find you can vary the tone and loudness of the pop by varying air pressure, and the angle and speed of your finger.

Place tip of finger between lips and puff out cheeks

THE FILL'ER UP

To make the sound of opening a bottle and pouring out its contents, combine the Champagne Pop with the Ploit (described on page 31). The "pop" is immediately followed by a quick series of ploits, starting with low tones and rising to higher ones. With the Fill'er Up, you can create the effect of soft drink commercials in your own living room.

THE CHAMPAGNE POP

Rap on hollow of cheek to produce a series of Ploits for the Fill'er Up

THE TONGUE FLOP

Ah, the Tongue Flop. One of those mouth sounds that most of us have made at one time or another. It is a simple sound that requires little vocal technology.

INSTRUCTIONS

1. Place your tongue on the roof of your mouth.

2. Tense your tongue a little, and pull it away from the roof of your mouth as you drop the jaw to create a slight vacuum.

3. Continue pulling the tongue away and dropping your jaw a bit. Your tongue should flop down on the floor of your mouth with a resonant "plop." (Record)

SUGGESTIONS

In all honesty, the Tongue Flop does not have many applications. But what can you expect from such a simple "plop"? You can, however, change the pitch of your Tongue Flops to simulate the "clip-clop" of a horse's hooves in a western song. (Record)

Jaw descends pulling tongue off roof of mouth

Shape your mouth as if you were saying "o." This will increase the resonance and volume of your "plop."

With practice, you can change the shape of your mouth to enable you to tongue-flop a musical scale. Try flopping "Yankee Doodle" and "On Top of Old Smokey." Teach several friends to tongue-flop "Happy Birthday to You" and then use the chorus of tongue-floppers to serenade birthday wishes to a friend.

THE COWBOY TONGUE FLOP

THE SLAP POP

The Slap Pop is a dynamic way to make a point or cap off an inciteful comment. It is a startingly loud pop that is sure to surprise anyone.

INSTRUCTIONS

1. While breathing through your nose (which causes the back of your mouth to be closed off from your throat), shape your mouth as if you were saying "o."

2. Do not tense your lips. Keep them loose. Take one hand, with fingers together, and lightly slap your lips.

3. Practice and experiment slapping softer and then harder, using different lip tension and mouth shapes. (Record)

SUGGESTIONS

Enter into a discussion or, better still, an outright argument with someone. When you have had your say, lean forward and slap-pop in his face. To your opponent, this is the verbal equivalent of slamming a door in his face.

Rear of mouth is closed to form resonant chamber

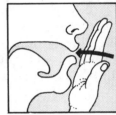

Hand strikes loose, "o"-shaped lips

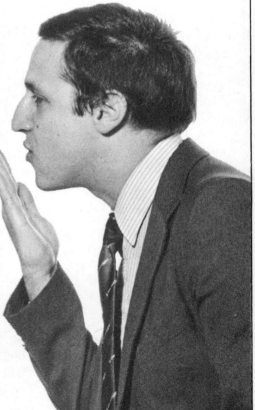

THE SLAP POP

PING-PONG POPS

Ping-Pong Pops are just that—pops that simulate a hard fought game of Ping-Pong. For all who have hung around YMCAs or recreation rooms, Ping-Pong Pops are a must.

THE PING-PONG SHOWDOWN

INSTRUCTIONS

1. Place your tongue midway back on the roof of your mouth.

2. Tense the tongue, pulling it away from the roof of the mouth to create a slight vacuum.

3. Continue tensing the tongue until you break the vacuum and create a "pop." This is the basis for the Ping-Pong Pop.

4. To get the "ping" and the "pong" sounds, alter the shape of your mouth to change the resonance: the "ping" will be the normal click-like "pop" you made from steps 1 to 3. For the "pong," hold your mouth as if you were saying "o."

5. Alternate the "ping" sound, with the more hollow "pong" sound. (Record)

Timing and rhythm are as important in the imitation as they are in the game. Actually, the "pong" sound always precedes the "ping." Make a quick "pong, ping," pause, and then another "pong, ping." You have a championship match.

SUGGESTIONS

If you work at it, this can be a very realistic imitation. Walk up to an ordinary table or desk, holding your invisible paddle, and begin playing. Imagine standing face-to-face against a steely-eyed opponent. Start your imitation and play vigorously—even chase the ball across the room as it bounces out of play. If your friends are willing, you can even play doubles.

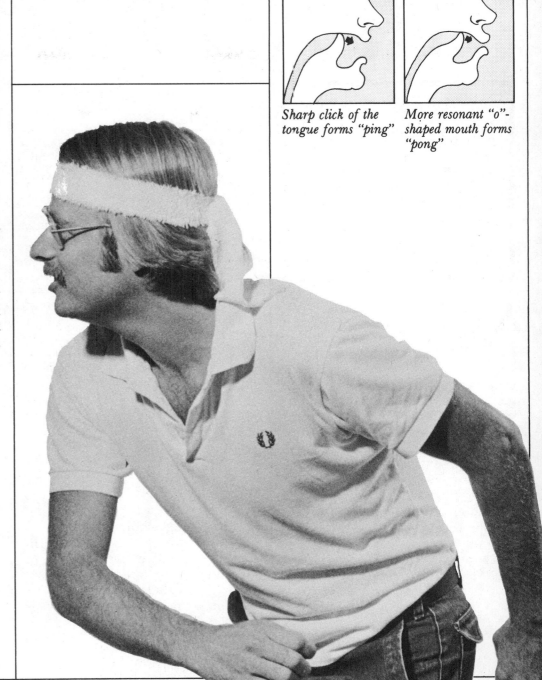

Sharp click of the tongue forms "ping"

More resonant "o"-shaped mouth forms "pong"

THE GLOTTAL FRY

CLICKS

Clicks are sharp, slight sounds that often go unnoticed. They are simple, undemanding noises that give us clues about actions around us. A click can be as significant as a phone disconnection or a door latching shut in a mystery movie—or as mundane as the sound of a toenail being clipped.

Scientists who dabble in the field of vocal production invented the term "glottal fry" years ago to describe a particular clicking sound produced in the glottis—the opening between the vocal folds in the upper part of the larynx. They are to be commended on this term, for indeed the Glottal Fry sounds exactly as though someone were frying an egg-over-easy in your throat. It is a fine sound that should become a basic effect in your vocal gadget bag.

INSTRUCTIONS

1. Relax. Sit back in your favorite easy chair. Kick off your shoes.

2. Open your mouth wide and say a long, steady "aah" in a low, relaxed tone.

3. Gradually lower the pitch and volume of this "aah" sound until the "aah" becomes a series of low, clicking or popping sounds. You are now officially frying your glottis in the short-order diner of your throat. (Record)

SUGGESTIONS

While glottal-frying, practice opening your throat and mouth as wide as possible to increase resonance and volume. Change the shape of your mouth from an "aah" sound to an "eee" sound. You should hear a change in tone. If you reverse this sequence, moving slowly from an "eee" to an "aah," you have the creaking of a castle door opening in a low-budget horror movie.

Continuing your glottal fry, form the mouth as if you were saying, in an exaggerated manner, the word "wow." You should be able to click out the sound of "wow" as the resonance of the mouth changes. With practice, you can use the Glottal Fry to talk in a fashion resembling that of an unearthly computer voice.

THE INHALED FRY

The Inhaled Fry has a much more full and resonant tone than the regular fry because it echoes more deeply in the chest.

1. Produce the Glottal Fry; then inhale at the same time so that you make a similar vocal-fry sound while drawing in air.

2. Open your throat wide as if to sing the lowest note you can. To increase resonance, form your mouth as if you were making an "o" sound. This configuration will give your Inhaled Fry its deepest, fullest, and loudest sound. (Record)

Practice articulating words in this full voice. You will sound very much like a Hollywood version of an interstellar alien.

*Mouth and throat
are opened wide*

THE
GLOTTAL
FRY

THE HICCUP

Many people like to think of the hiccup as God's little joke on the higher vertebrates. The notorious hiccup (or hiccough in polite circles) plagues not only mankind, but all mammals from time to time.

The hiccup knows no social boundaries, striking rich and poor alike without warning, reducing its victims to a helpless mass of "hics" and apologies. We are all particularly vulnerable to a hiccup attack during any suitably inconvenient time, such as a quiet prayer service, dinner with the boss, or just as the officer leans in your car and asks, "Have you been drinking?"

No one knows exactly what causes hiccups but they begin with the sudden involuntary contraction of the diaphragm. This results in forceful inhalation of air and the familiar snaplike closing of the glottis.

The cures are numerous, and all about equally ineffective. The simplest method is breathing slowly and deeply into a paper bag until you see stars. The most inventive cure, perhaps, is that of leaning over and drinking water out of the far lip of a glass. It is messy . . . hic . . . awkward and probably dangerous, but grandmothers . . . hic . . . swear by it.

Hic . . . damn.

THE TRIPLE CLICK

The Triple Click is an impressive set of three clicks that are produced in rapid succession. Once mastered, the clicks can be used to imitate anything from the sound of Fred Astaire's dazzling tap shoes to the hoofbeats of Genuine Risk.

INSTRUCTIONS

Click one:

1. Breathing through your nose, close your lips and place the front of your tongue just behind your bottom front teeth. The back of the tongue is arched upward to touch the roof of the mouth. A small air pocket should form between your tongue and the front roof of your mouth.

2. Abruptly push your tongue forward to drive out the pocket of air. This will make a pop or click by blowing the lips slightly apart. (The portion of the tongue just behind the tip should arch against the upper teeth and roof of your mouth.) Practice this until you can make the click easily. (Record)

Click two:

1. After click one, your tongue will be far forward and your lips very slightly apart.

2. Now with a sucking motion, abruptly pull the tongue back, drawing in just a bit of air so that the lips snap closed. This is click two.

3. Practice pushing and pulling the tongue back and forth to produce clicks one and two. Note that the tongue moves only slightly forward and backward to create the clicks. (Record)

Click three:

1. Once you are comfortable with click one and two, add a simple smack by pulling your lips slightly apart with a bit of a vacuum to make a slight, subtle smack. This is your third click. (Record)

This process may seem complex but it is simple to do—with practice. Produce each step in sequence, slowly. After click three, start over with click one. Be patient. Triple clicks will probably require a few trial-and-error sessions to become facile.

TOP HAT AND TRIPLE CLICKS

SUGGESTIONS

Horse Gallops. Use your Triple Click to imitate a galloping horse. Rhythm, here, is important. Emphasis should be on click one with the other two following quickly and smoothly in a "One, two, three, one, two, three" fashion. (Record)

To simulate a horse canter, use only click one and two in a four-beat sound. The rhythm should be "one-two, one-two—pause—one-two, one-two—pause."

Fred Astaire Taps. When you can do the Triple Click with ease, you will be able to sound out amazing tap-dance routines with your mouth. Practice by varying the rhythms of the clicks. (Record)

Make your clicks as accompaniment to records or radio. Better still, hum your favorite tap-dance tunes while you click out the taps. This hum-and-tap is an impressive effect. Try such standards as "Tea for Two," "Swanee River," or "Moonlight Bay."

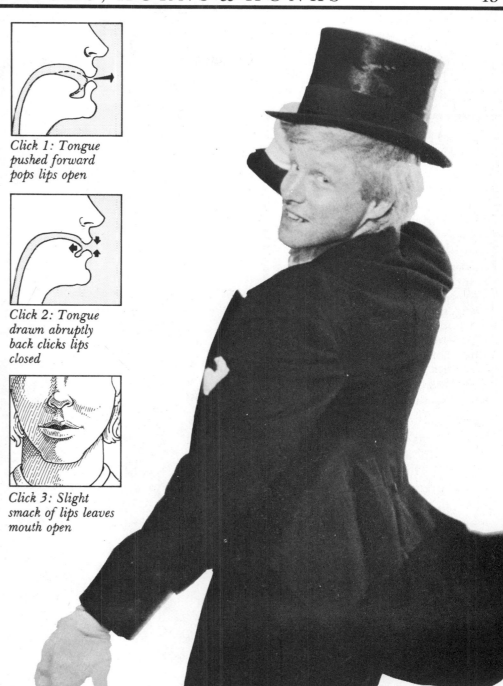

Click 1: Tongue pushed forward pops lips open

Click 2: Tongue drawn abruptly back clicks lips closed

Click 3: Slight smack of lips leaves mouth open

THE HONK

HONKS AND HORNS

The metallic blasts of honks and horns form the backdrop of our cities. The honk is that flat burst of sound that issues forth from the throats of squeeze-bulb bicycle horns and taxi cabs. The horn, on the otherhand, is the upper class version of the honk. (Apparently, one "honks" a Volkswagen bug and "sounds the horn" of a powder blue diesel Mercedes.) Depending on execution, honks and horns can vary from courteous beeps to jarring, acoustic assaults.

There is something in the quality of a Honk that is downright humorous. That is why both you and Harpo Marx can use it to great effect.

INSTRUCTIONS

1. Open your mouth and throat wide.

2. With a burst of exhaled air, produce a low-pitched, breathy "hhhaa." (The "a" should sound like the "a" in the word "back.") (Record)

The Honk should be aggressive, loud, and full. Practice this.

SUGGESTIONS

Use the Honk to punctuate your conversation. As you produce the Honk, hold your hand in front of you and make a suggestive squeezing motion with it.

The Honk can be used to initiate a range of sounds from a kid's tricycle horn to the blast of a tractor-trailer.

THE BASIC GOOSE

If you can make your voice break, begin the Honk in a falsetto and let it break quickly into a loud, low voice. (Record).

Mouth and throat are opened wide

SQUEEZING OFF A HONK

OCEAN LINER BLAST

The Ocean Liner Blast is a rich sound. Although not particularly useful, it is certainly impressive and lends exotic mystery and intrigue to any get-together.

INSTRUCTIONS

1. Put your lips together fairly tight in a very slight pucker.
2. Blow air through your lips to cause a slight vibration. Only the point where the lips touch should vibrate. You will have to experiment with the tension of your lips and your blowing pressure.
3. Produce a low, resonant hum as you blow out air to make your lips vibrate slightly. (Record)

SUGGESTION

Your Ocean Liner Blast should sound exactly like the real thing. Use it to simulate cold misty nights on the waterfront. If you let your hum fade away slowly, you will have the sound of a great luxury liner moored in the harbor distance.

Blow through tight lips for a buzz and then add hum

THE OCEAN LINER BLAST

TUGBOAT BLAST

As they plow the waterways of our great harbors, tugboats signal to the world with their loud, comic blasts. In the pilothouses of those little waterfront workhorses, their captains must snicker each time they yank the cord to produce the mechanical mating call.

Your Tugboat Blast can be a startling attention-getter, perfect for stealing the show at parties or destroying the tedium of a dull sociology lecture.

Do not be discouraged if you cannot make the tugboat sound immediately. It is not an easy sound to master and will probably take several sessions.

INSTRUCTIONS

1. Poke out your lower lip and press it firmly over and against your tensed upper lip. The inside bottom of your lower lip should be held tightly against the lower, outside edge of your upper lip. (If you glance in the mirror, you will look like Sir Winston Churchill.)

2. Blow air out so that the bottom lip vibrates in a kind of dirty "raspberry" sound. (You may find it helpful to concentrate the vibration slightly to one side of your mouth.) Practice until you can produce a strong buzzer-like sound.

3. Tense your lips and blow harder to increase the pitch of your buzz. Relax your lips a bit and reduce air pressure to lower the buzz. Work at this until you have some control over the pitch of the buzz.

4. Combine a strong, low hum at the same pitch of your lip buzz to create a loud controlled blast. (Record)

THE TUGBOAT BLAST

SUGGESTIONS

After you are able to produce a strong blast, try making the classic two-tone tugboat horn with a high blast followed immediately by a very low blast. Cup your hands over your mouth to muffle the sound a bit. (Record)

The combined hum-and-buzz necessary for the Tugboat Blast is a very versatile sound. You can adapt the basic hum-and-buzz so that it becomes a fire alarm, a penalty buzzer, or the signal for the booby prize on "Let's Make a Deal."

Lower lip protrudes so that inside edge touches upper lip

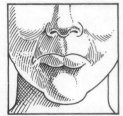

Hum and blow out, vibrating lower lip

ANIMAL SOUNDS

Most of us grow up against a bark-and-meow backdrop of pets—or we at least complain about those of our neighbors. Even in this modern age, animal sounds surround us.

We may or may not live within earshot of a barnyard, but we are all subjected to an array of animal sounds through Hollywood's vision of the world. What would Tarzan be without the chant of exotic birds and the roar of lions? What self-respecting movie about rural America could there be without crickets filling the evening air? And who could imagine a classic spring romance without birds twittering under soft dialogue?

Animal sounds set the stage. They create mood. They entertain. They can give that dull cocktail party or classroom just the lift it needs. One well-timed croak of a frog can transform any room into a veritable swamp.

THE PRINCIPLES OF ANIMAL SOUNDS

The Inhale: You can best approximate the vocal style and resonance of the animal by producing sounds as you *inhale*—this is quite different from normal speech produced when you *exhale*. Try speaking the first few letters of the alphabet in a normal voice. Then speak the same few letters, but *inhale* as you speak each one.

The inhaled voice sounds different from your normal voice and may be difficult to control at first. Practice saying short sentences in this "back talk," and then try singing high notes down to low notes. Production of these inhaled low notes are important for many of the animal sounds that follow.

The Stanislavski School of Animal Sounds:
The Stanislavski method of animal imitation
holds that if you wish to sound like an
animal, you must think like one. (Rumor
has it that the great Stanislavski himself
enjoyed woodchuck imitations in the
privacy of his bathroom.)

For many, thinking like an animal is not
difficult to do. Stand in front of a mirror.
Imagine yourself as furry, hoofed, and
horned. Now try to think like a cow about
the pleasures of the pasture. Then try for
a moment to empathize with an elephant.
Such exercises will add depth and
perspective to your animal imitations.
When you make animal sounds, mentally
crawl inside the animal and use your
entire body to act out the creature.
Who knows? You might find that
you were never cut out to be
human after all.

THE RANGE OF ANIMAL VOICES

We humans get pretty cocky as we sit atop the evolutionary heap with our sophisticated brains and voice mechanisms. Admittedly, plants are fairly quiet. But we often underestimate the subtlety, range, and flexibility of animal voices.

Take your basic chicken. Though not the Einstein of the animal kingdom, the chicken has a vocabulary of at least twenty-eight different calls, and that does *not* include swear words. The cheeping of hatching chicks, for instance, is used to communicate with other chicks in the brood so that all the chicks emerge from their eggs at the same time. The rooster crows for his territory and superiority, while the mother hen clucks incessantly to keep all her baby chicks together. Chickens have a particular squawk to announce that an egg is laid and an excited cluck when it is feeding time. Almost all birds have equally complex if somewhat more beautified systems of vocal communication.

Lower animals, too, have evolved voices

for communication. The Californian singing fish, for example, in a process similar to that of a croaking frog, uses a compartmentalized air bladder to produce a call under water.

Insects are able to produce a wide range of sounds, from the quiet whine of mosquitoes to the buzz of grasshoppers. But, the supreme vocalist of the insect world is the cicada. The male cicada sings in a loud, shrill buzz, produced by rapid contractions of a powerful muscle that causes a hard plate to vibrate. The resultant "sexual buzz" is used to attract female cicadas for miles. (The human male should be so lucky.)

Many insects (and even some fish) produce calls by rubbing parts of their bodies together in a process called stridulation. Very high-pitched, clicking sounds of grasshoppers and crickets can exceed man's ability to hear by almost five times.

Bats and porpoises produce ultrasonic impulses in their throats and are able to guide themselves by listening to the echoes of their own sounds.

THE DOG BARK

Man's best friend? Well, not exactly. Dogs used to be those furry little things that bark, lick your face, eat table scraps and cost only five dollars—if you were not given one free from the folks down the street.

Well, that's all changed. Sometime in the early 1960s, dogs formed a union to upgrade their quality of life. The result is that dogs still bark and lick your face—at their convenience—but they now are fed Burger 'n' Egg, flavored meat patties, cost hundreds of dollars, and

THE SPRINGER SPANIEL

insist on dragging city folk for a walk twice a day. These cagey canines have managed to market their big brown eyes very well.

You can go a long way with dog barks and whines. The sheer "cuteness" of imitation doggie barks is guaranteed to tug at the heartstrings of nearly everyone.

INSTRUCTIONS

1. The Dog Bark is an animal sound that should be produced while inhaling. In a normal—but low—voice, make a long "errr" sound.

2. Now say the same "errr" sound while inhaling. You should get a deep, guttural "errr." Practice this lead-in to the bark a few times.

3. Make the inhaled "errr" sound again, but this time (while still inhaling) extend the "errr," into a "ruff!" You will now have a "errr-ruff!" As you make the quick "ruff," your voice should rise very sharply in pitch. (Record).

That's the Dog Bark. Practice it, keeping in mind how your favorite pooch greets you. To imitate large vicious dogs, lower the pitch of the "errr-ruff," pulling it farther down in your throat. For those pesky smaller dogs, raise the pitch of the bark and produce it high in your throat.

SUGGESTIONS

The Dog Bark has two basic uses. One is the create-havoc-in-the-classroom bark. A Dog Bark in any location where dogs are traditionally frowned upon is sure to divert attention away from the subject at hand—be it a pop quiz, a boardroom lecture, or a violin concert.

The second use of the bark is to torment unsuspecting dogs. With all the power that dogs wield in our homes, this seems to be perfect poetic justice. As a little mutt is resting quietly, produce a quick bark. Nine times out of ten the dog will immediately bounce to its feet and rush to the door or window. You have every right to feel smug. Common sense dictates this decoy bark be used only on small dogs—Dobermans may be little less forgiving than Cockapoos.

Inhaling through slightly opened mouth

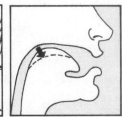
Tongue movement during "err-ruff"

THE PUPPY WHINE

As far as getting what you want is concerned, the Puppy Whine is the next best thing to begging on your knees. A much underused sound, the Puppy Whine is quite easy.

INSTRUCTIONS

Close your mouth and make, in your finest and highest falsetto, a short series of whining sounds. For each whine start very high, and then let the whine slide down a few notes in pitch. (Record)

SUGGESTIONS

The Puppy Whine is sure to melt the hardest of hearts—especially the female variety. Kids can whine for extra cookies from Mom. Secretaries can whine for higher raises, and dewy-eyed suitors can whine for more *amor*. Certainly the whine is more elegant than pleading, and at least gets you credit for originality.

THE PUPPY WHINE

THE COW MOO

Cows are not bright. For higher vertebrates, they are considered slow learners. This is the reason you never see trained-cow acts in the circus, as you do novelty dog acts and chimps on tricycles. No. Cows are milk machines, content to laze around in the sun. Knowing this, your cow imitations should reflect this slow, accepting, bovine attitude.

Contrary to cherished myths, cows do not really "moo." They have no "m" sound. Cows really say "ooo," but children's authors have plotted during the years to keep this from the public.

INSTRUCTIONS

1. Keep your mouth closed. Hum a moderately low, strong tone. Then, immediately, breathe through your nose to produce a strong *inhaled* hum. This backwards hum forms the basis of your cow imitation. Practice until you can produce a strong, low backwards hum.

2. Keeping your mouth closed, think of a low "ooo" sound as you make your inhaled hum. Let the inhaled "ooo" rise and fall in loudness and then trail off at the end, just as a good Guernsey would. (Record)

SUGGESTIONS

Like our friend the cow, be sure to affect a vacuous smile and stare vacantly into space when you moo. It is appropriate to moo politely before you down a glass of milk, or whenever you find yourself herded into a line such as at the theater, a concert, or the football season opener.

At your next party, teach several guests to moo. Why not get down on all fours and moo. (Warning! There may be lawsuits if some of the guests are milked.)

The Contented Cow

THE CAT MEOW

For centuries, cat owners around the world have projected affection and all manner of personalities on to their feline friends. Cats have been coddled and cuddled. They have been catered to and Little Friskied to the point where they even inherit fortunes.

But through it all, cats remain aloof, noncommittal, and downright arrogant. Even the familiar "meow" means "drop dead" in cat language.

The "meow" could more accurately be called "weow," for that is more precisely the sound cats make.

To capture the essence of cat, your "meows" or "weows" must reflect a condescending, disinterested, and blasé tone.

INSTRUCTIONS

1. With your highest falsetto, pronounce a soft, high-pitched "weow" that is very nasal. (If you hum a high note with your mouth closed, you will feel the sound high in your nasal passages. This nasal quality should be in your cat "weow.") The back of your tongue should be arched upward so that more sound is thrown into the nose.

2. Exaggerate and draw out the "weow" so that it's more like "we-owwww." (Record)

SUGGESTIONS

If you happen to be eloping by ladder, a soft cat "weow" makes a good signal that will not waken the snoring father of the house.

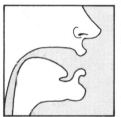

Tongue arched upward for added nasal tone

THE CAT MEOW

THE PIGEON COO

Pigeons are stout birds that stroll around in parks and other public places. They hang out on rooftops and window ledges and congregate at the feet of old ladies. Among fowl, pigeons are the urban welfare recipients.

From their refined and respected cousins, the doves, pigeons have acquired a sophisticated "coo." The Pigeon Coo has come to be one of the warmest and most congenial animal voices.

INSTRUCTIONS

1. Make a soft "ooo" sound in breathy, moderately high falsetto. Repeat this "ooo" in short, repeated fashion.

2. To really sound pigeon-like, produce a tongue-flutter with the "ooo." The tongue-flutter is made the same way one rolls an "r" in Spanish—by placing the tongue on the roof of the mouth and blowing out air over it so that it flutters. Practice this flutter.

3. Combine the soft "ooo" and the tongue-flutter to make a muffled "coo." The tongue-flutter can be continuous, but let the coos rise and fall in a series. (Record)

SUGGESTIONS

If there was ever a sound of affection, this is it. You have no doubt seen birds "bill and coo." (Due to a lack of lips, birds "bill" instead of kiss.) As they bill, they "coo" showers of affection on each other.

You can do the same thing. Run your beak against the neck of an acquaintance and "coo" softly. Guaranteed to either start or stop a friendship very quickly.

Lips shaped for an "ooo" sound

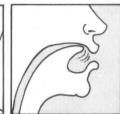
Tongue-flutter is added to falsetto "ooo"

THE COO

THE CHICKEN CLUCK

The chicken—not the dog—is man's best friend. Chickens have blessed us with feathers for our pillows, Eggs Benedict, and Colonel Sanders. We have chicken jokes, chicken cartoons, chicken toys, and Chicken Tetrazzini. What dog has ever given his life for the sake of our dinner tables?

Yet for all their nobility and self-sacrifice, chickens are funny. But don't think *chickens* don't know how funny they are. They chuckle when they "cluck" and jerk their heads around after a good prance around the barnyard. Chickens just do all those foolish things to entertain themselves.

The Chicken Cluck is *the* sound for attention-getting. It is as essential for party pranksters as rubber chocolates and poo-poo cushions.

INSTRUCTIONS

1. With a nasal falsetto, make a raspy "bok, bok, bok" sound. Keep your cheeks loose and, as you produce each "bok" allow your cheeks to fill with air and then collapse. The "boks" should have a sort of hollow, percussive sound.

2. After you master the "boks," add a "bo-ak" to the end. Let your

THE CHICKEN PRANCE

Allow cheeks to puff out loosely . . .   *. . . and then collapse*

voice soar up in pitch on the final "ak." Vary the pace of your "bok, boks" so that some are drawn out and others are clipped. (Record).

SUGGESTIONS

The classic chicken impression is for anyone who attends raucous birthday bashes, Saturday night fraternity parties, and out-of-control backyard barbecues.

Bend your arms and insert your thumbs into your armpits. These are your chicken wings. Arch your back, throw out your chest, and turn your head from side-to-side in short, jerky motions. Make your chicken cluck and scratch at the ground with your feet. *Bok-ak!*

Transform your appearance by stretching a pair of red gym shorts over the top of your head to become a rooster.

THE TURKEY GAA-LAA

Thanksgiving turkey has long been a prominent symbol in the United States. Our feathered friend has stood for the noble tradition of Colonial America, hard work, and the American custom of over-eating on holidays.

More recently, however, the turkey has come to be associated with anything that fowls up: false starts, misfires, or runs over budget. It is in this light that you can use the Turkey Gaa-laa, time and time again.

INSTRUCTIONS

1. Say "gaa-laa, gaa-laa" in a nasal falsetto. This is your fundamental turkey sound.

2. Place the index finger and thumb of one hand gently on either side of your larynx (Adam's apple) about midway up your neck.

3. As you say "gaa- laa, gaa-laa," rapidly (but gently) vibrate the larynx with an up-and-down motion of the hand. This will give a quick vibrato effect. Practice repeating "gaa-laa, gaa-laa" in quick succession. Let your voice trail off at the end, but continue your manual vibrato until the "gaa-laa" has completely stopped. (Record)

SUGGESTIONS

The "gaa-laa, gaa-laa" sound is probably the most effective and least subtle way to call someone a turkey. You can use the rallying cry to single out nerds, wimps, weenies, klutzes, creeps, and bozos whose actions qualify them for Turkey-dom.

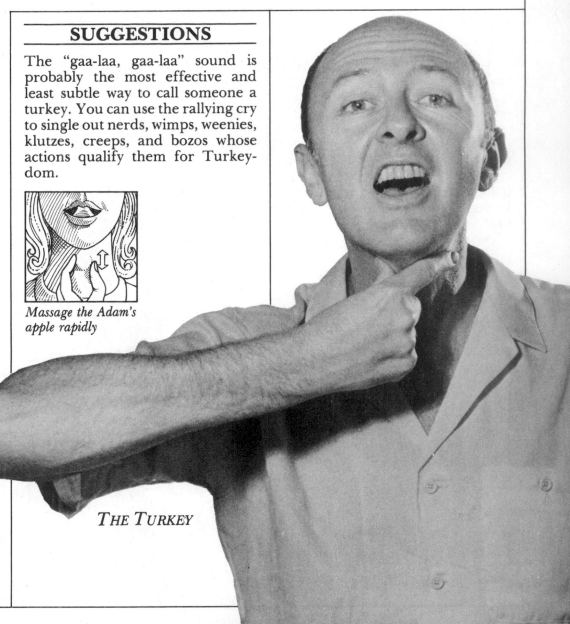

Massage the Adam's apple rapidly

THE TURKEY

THE PIG OOO-WEE

Pigs are overweight because they eat constantly and are not under pressure to fit into swimsuits in the summer. They have a good life. They root and snort around in mud with other pigs and bask in the sun on off days. (In the animal world, this is the equivalent of a desk job.)

But no pig with an ounce of porcine pride has ever uttered an "oink." Oink? An "oink" sounds more like the charming call of some long-legged bird, than the snort of a four hundred-pound ham.

No. Pigs grunt out a slovenly "oo-wee."

INSTRUCTIONS

1. Produce the Inhaled Glottal Fry (see page 40).

2. As you make a deep and resonant inhaled fry, shape your mouth so that you pronounce a slow "ooo-weee." Repeat over and over, shortening and quickening the pace of the "oo-wees."

3. Once you are comfortable with the "oo-wees," vary their loudness and pacing. Occasionally, emphasize and hold the "wee" longer, at other times emphasize the "ooo."

As you pronounce the "wee" let your Inhaled Glottal Fry rise in pitch for a more realistic grunt. Work toward a series of sporadic and varying "ooo-wees." (Record)

SUGGESTIONS

Pig snorts are always fine form just as you sit down at the table at a dinner party, and during the meal, they lend an air of festive abandon.

If you really get into pig "ooo-wees," get down on all fours and lower your head to root under such things as sofa cushions or bedcovers.

All of us have been, at one time or another, chastised by our mothers for the room "looking like a pigsty." Maybe now you can give that phrase new meaning.

Mouth shaped like "o" to add resonance

PIGGING OUT

THE FLY BUZZ

As a rule, we have come to treat with disgust anything that buzzes. The kid in the barber's chair squirms under the buzz of the electric clippers. Last night's partygoer winces at the morning buzz of the alarm clock. There is something in a menacing hum that penetrates and provokes.

Of all the disquieting sounds around us, the most irritating is probably the buzz of the common housefly. Ounce for ounce, the housefly has a greater ability to ruffle our composure than any other speck of matter in the universe. That is exactly why the Fly Buzz is so much fun—you can bug the heck out of folks with it. The Fly Buzz strikes a primal nerve ending in almost everyone.

THE TAKEOFF

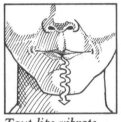

Taut lips vibrate with high buzz

INSTRUCTIONS

1. Press your lips together tightly.

2. Blow air out through your lips so that the center of your lips vibrates with a high buzz. This requires some experimentation. If you tighten your lips, the vibration rises in pitch; if you allow your lips to relax more, the pitch drops.

For the Fly Buzz you need a very high, thin buzz. (The humming buzz of bees, locusts, and electric shavers is somewhat lower.) Practice until you develop a clear, controlled buzz. (Record)

THE FLY IMPRESSION

Flies have never figured out window glass, and we all know that tormenting, persistent "fizz" they make as they struggle to fly through it. You can make that sound by producing your high buzz and then moving your lower jaw slightly, but rapidly, up and down. This changes the tension of your lips so that the buzz is broken into the scuffing sound of fly-against-glass.

With elbows bent and palms down, raise your hands up to the level of your shoulders. Rapidly flap these little hand-wings as you buzz. Doing your Fly Buzz, flit about the room, using short, quick steps. This is the basic fly.

THE LANDING

Do your best fly impersonation. Flit about the room, tilting and veering until you come to open wall space.

When it is time to land, face the wall and buzz your way right into it. Just as you hit, raise your right arm and leg slightly to one side and flatten against the wall. (You will be balancing against the wall on one foot.) This gives the impression that you are adhering with your little suction feet. Stay motionless for a moment and then, while still flat, you can nervously clean your face with your hands, just as the housefly might.

As you can imagine, this impression goes down well at senior proms, office parties, stately art openings, and even in elevators. With the Fly Buzz alone, it is possible to irritate up to forty people at one time.

But be careful. Someone might follow your act with their impression of a gigantic fly swatter.

THE LANDING

THE CRICKET CHIRP

Crickets form Mother Nature's little glee club. Their evening sing-ins fill the air with chirping music. Although they do not really have the clear tenor voice of Jiminy Cricket, their song has soothed more people to sleep than Brahms' lullaby. The sound of crickets has come to be the epitome of a peaceful, country night.

INSTRUCTIONS

1. Form your mouth as in the Pucker Whistle (page 72). Practice until you can *inhale* through the pucker to make a clear whistle.

2. Work up a fair amount of saliva in your mouth. Tilt your head forward so that the pucker points downward.

3. As you inhale a clear whistle, adjust your tongue so that the air coming into your mouth (through the small opening of your pucker) bubbles through the saliva on your tongue. The bubbling of your inhaled whistle produces the rapid chirps of a cricket. (Record) Practice. The saliva should be kept between the middle of your tongue and the roof of your mouth. The air bubbling through it should keep it from moving too far toward the front of the mouth. Produce

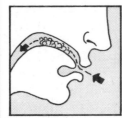

Inhaled air over saliva breaks whistle into chirps

Puckered lips produce inhaled whistle

the cricket chirps in gentle waves of sound by inhale-whistling in rhythmical swells.

SUGGESTIONS

If you ever need to set the mood of the great outdoors, spray pine-scented air freshener around the room and make the cricket song. The sound can be so realistic that you can actually convince teachers that the little creatures are loose in algebra class.

Of course the natural time for cricket chirps is at night. Cut off the lights, sit in a warm tub, and create your own pond. Get that special someone to produce the Frog Croak (page 63) and you can have your own romantic, secluded lagoon.

BATHTUB CHIRPS

THE FROG CROAK

The frog is undoubtedly the most lovable amphibian. But frogs suffer from a bad reputation. All right, they may be cold and clammy, but they are not slimy, and it is not their fault if they have been dropped down the dresses of countless schoolgirls. Remember, it is the *toad* that is covered with all those warty things. Frogs have clearer skin than high school sophomores.

The frog is a stately old monarch. He croaks and "ribits" and sits on his lily-pad throne, snatching flies from the air with his Scotch-tape tongue. The frog croak is clearly one of the most noble of animal voices.

INSTRUCTIONS

1. Shape your mouth as if you were going to sing the very lowest "o" sound that you can. Your throat should be very open and your lips in an "o" shape.

2. Exhale a low "o" sound, then *inhale* the same low "o" sound to produce a very hollow, resonant but almost crackly sound. Practice this deep, guttural inhaled croak.

3. As you inhale the low tone, keep your throat very open and articulate a "wah" with your mouth. Draw the "wah" out longer to sound

Throat opened and mouth shaped like "o" sound to add resonance

THE CROAK

more like a frog and as you draw out the inhaled "wah," let the pitch of your croak glide upward just slightly. Try stringing several of these "wahs" together without stopping the croaking tone. (Record)

With some practice you should sound more and more like a frog. Once you have mastered the basic croak, you can do several frog variations. To make the classic "ribit" sound, produce your inhaled croaking sound and just inhale the word "ribit." Then try other frog favorites such as "breep" and "nee-deep."

SUGGESTIONS

The Frog Croak should be used with some discretion for it can easily be mistaken for an attack of gas. Try hunkering down into a crouch on all fours. Croak, and then lap your tongue out quickly, a few times.

Hopping on all fours and "nee-deeping" your way into a sales conference or biology class will get you points for creativity—but may also get you pithed and dissected.

THE LION GROWL

Lions are the superstars of the animal kingdom. With their impressive Farrah Fawcett hairdos, they have starred in innumerable grade-B movies and television series. Although they shy away from comedy roles, their heavy, dramatic parts have earned them an enviable reputation as "the Richard Burtons of the jungle." Your Lion Growls must always reflect this tradition of prideful showmanship.

THE LION

INSTRUCTIONS

1. Make the Inhaled Glottal Fry (see page 40). Open your throat as wide as possible to make the deepest and most resonant sound you can. Shape your mouth to make an "rrr" sound as you inhale, raising the back of the tongue upward to constrict the upper throat a bit. This will "pull" the "rrr" sound back farther in the upper throat.

Arched tongue moves downward during growl

2. Shift from this inhaled "rrr" to an inhaled "o" sound. You will have to drop the floor of your mouth and open your throat wider. Experiment with this growl. (Record)

To develop your own roar, start with the growl on a higher note. As you move from an "rrr" to an "o" sound, let your growl slide to lower notes.

SUGGESTIONS

Lion Growls can be combined with Elephant Trumpets (page 65) for your own portable jungle scenes.

Get out your old loincloth, and clench a butter knife between your teeth. (If you do not have a loincloth handy, Jockey shorts are acceptable.) Make a few Lion Growls. Imagine a nearby chair is a lion about to attack. Steely-eyed and poised, slowly tiptoe toward the chair. Like a striking cobra, make your heroic lunge. Roar and growl as you become locked in mortal combat.

Depending on where you stage it, this little act can get you several weeks vacation from the office, a trip to the school guidance counselor, dismissal from the armed forces, or a quick divorce.

ELEPHANT TRUMPET

This pachydermal pucker is a surefire hit at chic get-togethers, office parties, and Republican Conventions. A quick series of elephant trumpets is guaranteed to stop conversation dead as the room makes way for an elephant charge.

INSTRUCTIONS

1. Your lips should be dry and free of all lipstick, suntan lotion, and motor oil. Tuck your lips in, with the upper lip slightly over the lower lip. Keep lips very taut.

2. Fill your cheeks with air so that they and the areas above and below your lips billow out. (The corners of your mouth should be held in tightly as if you're trying to create dimples.)

3. Allow your upper lip to billow out slightly more than your lower lip. Forcefully blow out air so that the lips vibrate, making a squealing sound. Continue to try variations, working to produce a full-sounding trumpet that rises and falls in pitch—exactly like an elephant cry. (Record)

The sound alone is not enough, however. You must add realistic trunk action. With your arm extended, place the inside of your elbow next to the side of your face. As you sound the elephant call, raise and lower your head and arm in the manner of a rogue bull elephant.

You now have a first-class elephant mating call.

SUGGESTIONS

You can add dimension to your elephant calls by grunting a Tarzan-like "Un-gowa, Nimba" (Ün gòw'e Nümbe) before each trumpet. And herds of elephants become a reality with five or more skillful elephant callers. Imagine the fun of trampling your friend's living room in a frenzied stampede.

Taut lips held in tightly   *Allow areas above and below lips to billow*

HERD OF ROGUE ELEPHANTS

WHISTLES

Whistles are the shrill signals of the world. They warn. They mark. They urge. They entertain. The toy train whistles its way around the crouching six-year-old. The teakettle beckons us to the kitchen. Tons of clanking machinery become silent at the jarring blast of the factory whistle. And street-corner greasers two-finger whistle their approval of the well-endowed passerby.

Whistles are authority. White-gloved policemen tame traffic with a frantic semaphore of waves and whistles, while lifeguards and potbellied gym teachers twirl their little silver symbols of power at the end of shoelace lanyards.

WHISTLING WIZARDRY

Most of us consider whistling a musical novelty, best reserved for the privacy of home and family. From time to time, we are all subjected to the overly cheerful public whistler who performs gratis in checkout lines, crowded buses, and bank lobbies. The occasional whistler in amateur talent competitions seems to be little more than a "Gong Show" dropout. For some reason, whistling performances are viewed as talent misdirected or gone astray.

But, over the years, the art of whistling has surfaced occasionally to bask briefly in the rays of the public limelight. In the early 1900s, vaudeville had its share of novelty whistlers. The great Al Jolson himself was a whistler of some renown.

In the 1930s a serious whistler, Fred Lowery, blew on the scene. Practicing whistling for four or more hours a day, Lowery developed unheard of muscular control and a musicianship uncommon to whistling. He teamed up with the orchestra of Horace Heidt in 1938 for a soulful rendition of "Indian Love Call" that sold well over a million records. Lowery went on to record works ranging from "Listen to the Mockingbird" to selections from Bach and Stravinsky. Blind himself, Lowery often performed with the blind pianist Alec Templeton.

In Walt Disney's 1938 classic film *Snow White and the Seven Dwarfs* seven little men in droopy hats endeared themselves to the American public with their tight whistling harmonies. The song "Whistle While You Work" rocketed into the hit parade.

Just after World War II, the masterful Elmo Tanner joined with the orchestra of Ted Weems for another whistling hit, "Heartaches." Whistling schools sprang up and even books were written on whistling, such as Agnes Woodward's *Whistling as an Art*. One Diana Dixon was declared by Robert L. Ripley ("Believe It or Not") to be the "World's Champion Woman Finger Whistler," with her three-and-a-half-octave range.

Julie Andrews made her bid for world-class whistler with her 1955 Broadway debut in the opening of *The Boy Friend*. In 1957, "The Colonel Bogey March," from the motion picture *The Bridge over the River Kwai*, had more Americans whistling than any other song in history.

About this same time, the bittersweet theme from the television show "Lassie" introduced millions of misty-eyed viewers to the weekly adventures of a boy and his collie with an IQ of 140. Television gave us the homespun theme of "The Andy Griffith Show," during which the folksy Griffith and his little cross-eyed son, Opey, skip stones across a pond. Also about this same time the genius of Toots Thielman pulled whistling into the idiom of jazz, with his classic jazz guitar and whistle-piece "Bluezette."

Of course, whistling has had its novelty luminaries. Horatio Q. Birdbath whistled and made all manner of noises for Spike Jones during a span of some twenty years. Simon Argevitch, a carnival and talk-show veteran, manages to eek out a whistle with nine cigars, five spoons, and six drinking straws in his mouth.

There are many serious whistlers too. Among the best known is probably Roger Whitaker. The international singer baritone talks his way through a range of standards—folk and popular songs. Jason Serinus (who changed his name to *Serinus*, a Latin classification of canaries) resides in San Francisco and regularly performs with symphony orchestras. His whistle is the warble of the bird Woodstock in the television animations of Charlie Brown.

Since 1977, there has been an annual Olympics of whistling known as the International Whistle-off in Carson City, Nevada. Whistling enthusiasts from all over the world converge for world-class competition in some six whistling categories. It is a mass rubbery-lipped celebration of the noble art of whistling.

Whistling will wax and wane in popularity. It may surface in the form of an elegant movie theme, a punk rock diversion, or a folk-song revival. But there is no doubt: Those penetrating, piping, and mysteriously compelling tones of the whistle will always be with us.

With a whistle, we summon the dog from our neighbor's flower bed. We whistle absentmindedly to kill time. We whistle while we work. The whistle has become the mainstay of all janitors, TV repairmen, and construction workers.

On dark streets, we quicken our pace and whistle confidently to buttress our sagging courage. By whistling, we can ignore. And, with arms draped behind us, we rock on our heels and whistle to pretend innocence.

Like no other single sound, the versatility of the whistle graces our world and enriches our communication.

THE WHISTLE PRINCIPLE: HOW WHISTLES WORK

The whistle has a characteristic shrill, clean tone marked by purity and simplicity. And yet the aerodynamics of whistle production are some of the most subtle and complex of any sound. Only recently have physicists begun to unravel the mysteries of the whistle.

Almost every sound around us is created

by the transfer of vibrations from some rapidly moving object to surrounding air molecules. In the case of the voice, our vocal folds vibrate, disturbing the air around them. The resulting vibrations travel in the air to the ears of others. In whistles, however, no physical object vibrates—the air molecules themselves vibrate directly.

All whistles, from puckers to piccolos, operate on the principle that when a steady stream of air is disturbed in a particular manner the turbulence produces a series of regularly spaced, swirling vortices of air. These spirals of air act as vibrating devices that produce the whistle tone.

In the whistle of a flute, for instance, the purity of tone is attributed to the fact that, unlike most other musical instruments, only the air itself vibrates to produce the remarkably "airy" tone of the flute.

LEARNING WHISTLES

Whistles are the most difficult and evasive mouth sounds to learn. Perhaps more than any other sound, mouth whistles require delicate coordinated manipulation of the tongue, teeth, lips, and sometimes fingers. For this reason, perfecting whistles requires more than the usual patience and practice to adapt the general rules to the peculiar structure of your own mouth.

Experimentation is necessary in developing your whistles. Adjust the lips. Try different air pressures. Move the tongue slightly. And always listen for hints of that elusive whistling sound. Take a break, and later try again.

Once you begin to hear a faint whistle, you are close to home. It will then be a matter of fine tuning.

THE PUCKER WHISTLE

PUCKER PRINCIPLE

The Pucker Whistle is produced by a principle known as the "whole tone effect," the same principle by which teakettles whistle.

The whistle is generated when a flow of air rushes against a small hole. Spirals of air form around the outer edges of the hole, setting up disturbances in the air flow. These minute eddies of air create sound vibrations as the air is forced through the opening, and a whistle tone is produced.

The loudness of the Pucker Whistle is determined by the speed of the airflow. Blowing harder makes a louder whistle.

The pitch (or how high or low the tone is) is determined by the size of the mouth cavity. Drawing the tongue back and lowering the floor of the mouth enlarges the mouth cavity and lowers the tone. Pushing the tongue forward and raising the floor of the mouth, on the other hand, shrinks the resonating mouth cavity and raises the pitch.

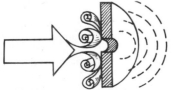

The Pucker Whistle is the most universal and useful member of the whistle family. Throughout history everyone from barons to buffoons has used it to signal, summon, and give vent to melody. As a ritual of childhood, most of us spent hours hyperventilating to perfect this elusive musical pucker.

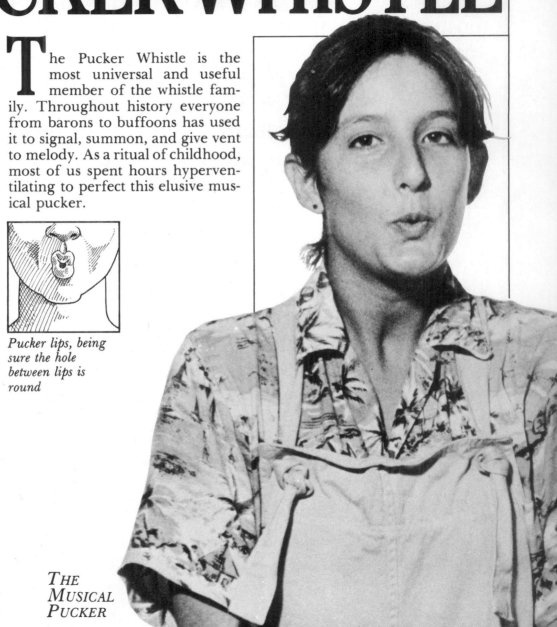

Pucker lips, being sure the hole between lips is round

THE
MUSICAL
PUCKER

INSTRUCTIONS

The whistle pucker comes quite naturally to some people but can be difficult for others. There are three basic variables involved: the tongue, the pucker, and the blowing of air.

1. Relax your tongue on the floor of your mouth, setting the front edge of it against the back of your bottom teeth.

2. Pucker your lips slightly. Do not exaggerate the pucker. All you really need to do is form a small round opening between the lips.

3. Blow, gently—as if you were romantically blowing out a lighted match in front of your lips. Blowing hard only distorts the Pucker Whistle. (Record)

If you have trouble producing a whistle, look in a mirror as you try. Open and close the small hole between your lips ever so slightly. Try tensing your lips into a more "pointed" pucker and vary your lip tension.

To lower the pitch, draw your tongue back slightly from the edge of your bottom teeth as you lower the floor of your mouth.

To raise the pitch, keep the front of your tongue against the bottom teeth and arch the back and mid-portions of the tongue upward, pushing the tongue farther forward in your mouth.

Try a musical scale and simple melodies, such as "Oh! Susannah" and "On Top of Old Smokey" before you go on to anything more complicated. Whistling is perfect for old standards and classical numbers but somehow lacks the "umph" necessary for disco and new wave.

VIBRATO

In whistling, the difference between rank amateur and seasoned professional is all a matter of vibrato—that subtle wavering of a note that gives it a fluid, schmaltzy sound.

To add vibrato to your whistle, keep your tongue against your bottom teeth. As you whistle a relatively high note, raise the mid-portion of your tongue very slightly by pushing it a little forward. Let it (and the floor of your mouth) rise and fall rapidly for a wavering effect.(Record)

This requires practice, but the resulting vibrato adds a romantic dimension to your whistling.

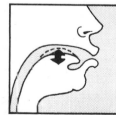

For vibrato, allow mid part of tongue to waver up and down

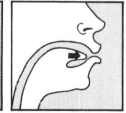

For Tongue Tippling, tongue is raised slightly off floor of mouth and eased back and forth

TONGUE TIPPLING

Tongue tippling is to Pucker Whistling what yodeling is to voice. By moving your tongue slightly, you can get a remarkably beautiful, abrupt change in the pitch of your whistle much like a whistled yodel. You should not try this until you are fairly confident in your whistling ability.

Instead of whistling with your tongue against your bottom teeth, whistle a note with the tip of your tongue pulled back from your teeth, off the front floor of your mouth. While whistling, delicately ease the tongue forward (keeping it above the floor of your mouth) until the tip touches the bottom lip just above your lower teeth. Practice this. You should work toward a sudden break in pitch.

Tongue tippling works by suddenly altering the shape of your mouth. When the tongue is held back and off the floor of the mouth, the resulting cavity under the tongue helps determine the pitch. When suddenly you seal off this cavity by touching your tongue against the inside of your bottom lip, you drastically alter the pitch-determining chamber of your mouth producing the abrupt break in notes.

Use Tongue tippling to imitate birds and to add baroque trills to your whistled songs. It is an elegant effect and well worth the practice and effort.(Record)

INVISIBLE WHISTLE

The sole purpose of the Invisible Whistle is to harass mankind. The Invisible Whistle is not particularly musical or versatile, but it *is* invisible. That one quality makes it useful for all sorts of sonic shenanigans.

INSTRUCTIONS

1. Place your tongue near the roof of your slightly opened mouth, allowing the edges of your tongue to form a seal against the inside, upper gums. The tip of your tongue should touch the roof about 1/8 to 1/4 of an inch behind your front teeth.

2. Draw back the very tip of your tongue just slightly from the roof of your mouth so that you make a small opening between the tongue and the roof. The sides of your tongue are still sealed against the gums.

3. *Very* gently, blow air over your tongue so that it escapes through the little hole you have just made. Adjust the tongue to subtly change the size and shape of the hole until you can hear a whistling sound. (Record)

Be patient. The whistle will be faint at first. You might try varying air pressure and raising and lowering your jaw slightly.

THE
INVISIBLE
WHISTLE

SUGGESTIONS

The shrill little whistle is not very loud but can be controlled to produce music. With your mouth just open and a blank expression on your face, you can produce the whistle quite invisibly. In confined spaces such as automobiles, elevators, classrooms, and religious services, you will find this whistle to be good entertainment. Confused people will furrow their eyebrows, and begin opening and closing windows, adjusting hearing-aid levels, and the like. Dogs are particularly put off by this. If you are clever enough to look serious, your whistle will go completely undetected.

Subtle public harassment can be a fine and rewarding hobby—particularly if you are not caught.

Tip of tongue drawn back slightly to form small hole

Tongue edge sealed on roof of mouth

THE TAXI WHISTLES

The Taxi Whistles and Hand Coos are produced by the physics principle of "edge tone." Many whistles are created by an edge tone when a rapidly moving stream of air rushes across an opening. The rush of air is directed at the "edge" of the opening in such a way that it sets up swirling eddies of air that disturb the airflow and generate whistling vibrations.

When we blow in a particular way across

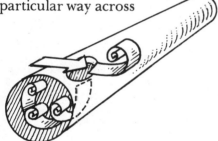

the opening of an empty bottle, this edge tone produces a low, steamship-like whistle. Flutes, recorders, pipe organs, and even police whistles operate on this principle of splitting a rushing airstream into swirls of air to make sound vibrations.

For the Fingerless Taxi Whistle, you hold your tongue and lips in such a manner that a cavity forms under the tongue, and a small hole is formed between the tip of the tongue and lower lip. As you channel rushing air across the hole with your tongue, you get a powerful edge tone—and a loud whistle.

In the case of the Hand Coo, you cup your hands to allow a hole to form between your thumbs. Inside is the cavity formed by your cupped hands. As you blow obliquely across the thumb hole you get the whistling coo. By changing the shape of the cavity, you can alter the reasonating body of air to raise and lower pitch.

DAIRY PRODUCTS AND YOUR WHISTLE

It is widely understood that a mouthful of soda crackers can put a damper on whistling. But, what is not generally known is that dairy products—notably milk, cheese, and yogurt—are the scourge of good whistling. Before a performance, a serious whistler will not touch a glass of milk or a grilled cheese sandwich. Such dairy products alter the saliva-and-mucus balance in the mouth and throat to make whistling, and even singing, difficult.

This is not to say avoidance of dairy products is encouraged. Dairy products are normally fine. But when you are backstage at the local talent show, about to make your whistling debut with "The Flight of the Bumblebee," you might give that milkshake a miss.

TWO-FINGER WHISTLE

The art of hailing a taxi is the urban equivalent of lassoing a galloping horse. It takes determination, patience, and a lot of savvy to pull down a checkered cab. You may plant yourself in strategic positions and wave on tiptoe, but the Taxi Whistle is by far the safest and most effective device yet invented to halt a speeding hack.

There are two kinds of Taxi Whistles—those requiring the use of fingers, and those using only the mouth. Both will require patience and practice, but diligence will be royally rewarded with an ear-piercing shrill that will lock the brakes of cabs at five hundred yards.

INSTRUCTIONS

1. Open your mouth and draw your lower lip tautly inward to cover the top of your lower teeth.

2. Flattening your tongue, bring it forward to hover above the inside edge of your bottom lip.

3. Touch the tips of your pinkie fingers together at the sides at an angle of about 90 degrees.

4. Nails upward, insert the tip of the "V" just under the tip of your tongue, rolling the tip of your tongue upward and back a bit. The tongue tip is curved upward, toward—but not touching—the front roof of the mouth.

5. Bring the upper lip down on the first joint of the pinkie fingers. There should be a triangle-like opening formed between the inside "V" of the fingers and the taut lower lip.

6. Blow fairly briskly, directing air over the tongue and down across the triangular opening. (No air should escape from the corners of your mouth.)

7. Experiment. Adjust the tips of your little fingers, moving them just slightly apart. Vary their angles. Try various tongue tensions. Looking into a mirror can be a helpful way to monitor your adjustments.

Be patient. It will take a few sessions. Listen for the faintest "grab" of a whistle and you will be on the right track. With practice you will soon be belting out decibels of shrill sound with this, the loudest method of whistling.

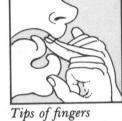

Tips of fingers inserted; tongue is folded back, lower lip very taut

"V"-shaped hole formed between fingers and lower lip

THE TWO-FINGER WHISTLE

FINGERLESS WHISTLE

The Fingerless Taxi Whistle is not an easy whistle to master. It will require practice and patient experimentation, but once captured it is the most convenient of loud whistles.

INSTRUCTIONS

1. Open your mouth and draw your lower lip tautly inward to cover the top edge of your lower teeth.

2. Flattening your tongue, bring it forward to seal against the inside edge of your lower lip. Make your tongue slightly "V"-shaped, lifting the sides up a bit as you draw back the very tip of your tongue so that you create a small hole between the tongue tip and the middle, inside edge of your lower lip. The resulting small hole between the lip and front of the tongue is critical. To form the hole properly, you must arch the tongue a little off the floor of the mouth as you draw back the tongue tip about 1/16 of an inch.

3. Close your mouth slightly. Keep your upper lip pulled high and your lower lip tensed and taut.

4. Blow fairly gently, directing air over the hole by adjusting the slight "V" of your tongue. As you blow, you will have to increase the tension of both lips.

Lower lip is very tightly drawn over lower teeth, with tongue lifted slightly off floor of mouth

Tongue is sealed against tight lower lip with tip withdrawn to form hole

THE FINGERLESS WHISTLE

SUGGESTIONS

Because the Fingerless Taxi Whistle does not require the use of hands, it makes an excellent warning for use when skating, bicycling, skate-boarding, skiing, and the like.

This whistle can also be used for all sorts of imitations. Birds, sirens, and even the sound of whining machinery can be coaxed out with the use of cupped hands.

HAND COOS

As any makeup-faced Hollywood Indian will tell you, Hand Coos have been the downfall of many a pioneering settler. Saturday afternoon westerns are crammed with Indians crawling around in the underbrush, cooing out ambush signals on their hands. Evidentally, Hand Coos and ambushes were once a popular pastime in the American West.

The sound of the Hand Coo is a cross between the woody softness of a recorder and the mellow ring of a dove. It is a gentle musical tone—a sound that will expand your whistle repertoire.

INSTRUCTIONS

1. Hold your opened hands, palms up, in front of you. Place one hand on top of the other, positioning the hands to overlap at right angles as in illustration A.

2. With the thumb and index finger of the bottom hand, encircle the fingers of the top hand at approximately the first knuckle as in illustration B.

3. Rotate the hand just encircled 90 degrees toward you. The fingers should rotate within the thumb and index finger of the other hand as in illustration C.

4. Allow the hand you just rotated to bend at the knuckles so that you can bring the thumbs of each hand together facing you. Adjust your hands so that they are comfortable, with an enclosed cavity inside the cup of your hands. Work at this until the hands seal this cavity completely. The only air space should be the hole between your thumbs as in illustration D.

5. Bend the thumbs at the top knuckle. (The thumbs should be symmetrical.) Place your upper lip on your thumbnails, cover the knuckles with your slightly opened mouth and blow down *across* the hole between your thumbs as in illustration E. Do not blow *into* the hole, but across it.

If the cavity is sealed and you are blowing across the hole formed by your thumbs, a cooing sound should blow forth. Try adjusting your hands. Pull them apart, shake them, and retrace the steps. Try different angles and speeds of blowing across the knuckle on your thumbs. With practice, the coo will come. (Record)

SUGGESTIONS

Once you can produce a fairly strong "coo," let the middle, ring, and little fingers of the outside hand flap out at the bottom knuckles to change the pitch of the Hand Coo. With a little work you can control this finger-flap to the point of playing songs. You will find that subtle changes with hand shape and speed of blowing can create new notes.

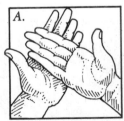

A. *Hands overlapped at right angles*

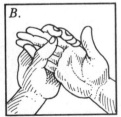

B. *Thumb and index finger encircle fingers of other hand*

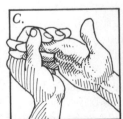

C. *Rotate the hand in encircled fingers 90 degrees so that thumb points up*

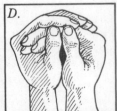

D. *Bend hand to place thumbs symmetrically together. Be sure there is an enclosed hollow within hands*

THE HAND COO

INDIAN HAND COO

The classic Indian ambush was always preceded by Hand Coos. You, too, can use the Indian signal in the office, the classroom, the library, or at a singles mixer.

Use the finger-flap described for the Hand Coos to change the pitch of your coo rapidly. Then trill your tongue (like a Spanish "r" sound) as you produce the Hand Coo. (Record)

In the school library, Indian Hand Coos can be utilized to signal "teacher's coming—get off the desks." If you are caught, cooing loudly, merely explain that you are demonstrating a poignant passage from *The Last of the Mohicans* for your schoolmates.

Similar Hand Coos make fine signals at crowded parties. You can prearrange meanings of various Hand Coo signals with a friend or partner. Then use the Hand Coo to inconspicuously signal across the room messages such as "check out that blonde by the punch bowl," or "let's blow this joint."

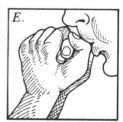

Place upper lip on thumbnails and blow down across hole between thumbs

THE DOUBLE WHISTLE

The Double Whistle is an amazing effect. By whistling out of the corners of your mouth, you can actually produce two whistle tones that can be used for harmonies or eerie effects.

Blow gently through two holes formed on either side of slightly pointed tongue

THE DOUBLE WHISTLE

INSTRUCTIONS

1. Open your mouth slightly, point your tongue, and stick the point of your tongue just through your lips. Your tongue should be somewhat stiff, and two small (1/8-inch) holes should be formed at the corners of your mouth.

2. Blow *very* softly, adjusting your lips and tongue until you can hear a bit of a whistle. This will probably take a few sessions, but keep trying. By diligence and experimentation, you will be able to produce a whistle from each side of your mouth simultaneously. (Record)

SUGGESTIONS

You can use the Double Whistle for harmony on songs. The Double Whistle has such a strange sound that it is almost impossible for your basic nearsighted office supervisor or teacher to locate. Many high school teachers, in fact, have been driven to early retirement with skilled use of the Double Whistle.

MUSICAL INSTRUMENTS

Music is basic to man. Before humankind could articulate words, our ape-like ancestors pounded rhythmically on logs to produce primitive music. Over eons of time, the voice developed, and with it, the incredible gift of singing evolved. Instruments were invented to extend and accompany the music of the voice. All manner of exotic percussion, stringed, and wind instruments came into being the world over.

The attempt of this chapter is to show that, even with centuries of evolution, musical instruments are still no match for the range and flexibility of the human voice. With a little practice, it is possible—with just our modest mouths—to out-strum the strings, out-blow the winds, and generally out-class the brass.

THE VIOLIN

The violin is the little stringed cigar box that sings in a most wondrous whine. More than any other instrument, there is a tradition and mystique to the violin that has followed it through history.

But do not let that bother you. Tossing away centuries of noble heritage, you can perform violin with your mouth—although it does not have the elegance of the real thing. Somewhere inside that dental work of yours lies a Stradivarius.

INSTRUCTIONS

1. Hold your lips nearly together, but slightly draw in your lower lip to allow your upper teeth to rest on it.

2. With your finest falsetto, hum a high note. Concentrate on projecting the note up and out through the small opening between your teeth and lower lip. This gives

A MOUTHSOUND STRADIVARIUS

your violin the correct tone.

3. Vibrato, that beautiful wavering of pitch and volume, takes some practice, but it will be well worth the effort. It is essential for good mouth violin. Push air upward from your stomach muscles and diaphragm and blow out so that it pulsates through your mouth. (Record)

SUGGESTIONS

The mouth violin is definitely a class act. As you produce the violin sound, cradle an imaginary violin with your chin and one arm, and bow the invisible instrument with your other hand while you sway elegantly from side to side. Be suave. Be ever-so delicate.

Use the mouth violin to serenade the love of your life over a fine meal of fast food, soft drinks and fries or, if you are more intrepid, at a fine restaurant.

Teeth on lower lip sharpen falsetto whine

VIOLIN PIZZICATO

The violin is not always bowed to produce its singing tone. Sometimes the strings are lightly plucked to make soft, percussive sounds. This plucking is called violin pizzicato.

Violin pizzicato has been an integral part of Western music for hundreds of years. From classical symphonies to elevator music, the pizzicato dances softly in the background of many major musical works. It was not until fairly recently, however, that the art of violin pizzicato reached its zenith, with its use for the sound of Daffy Duck on tiptoe as he sneaks across the silver screen.

INSTRUCTIONS

1. Produce a high falsetto tone as you say the syllable "ta." Emphasize the burst of the "t."

2. Now put your lips together, so that your bottom lip protrudes slightly. Continue saying your short "ts" in a falsetto. The percussion of each "t" should vibrate your bottom lip sharply to form the pluck of your pizzicato. Practice until you get a single, sharp "pluck" of your lip with each note. (Record)

3. Slowly, practice the musical scale. Then try faster scales and strains from any classical music that comes to mind.

Your violin pizzicato should be a rapid sequence of notes for best effect. Long, gliding, musical scales are excellent.

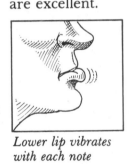

Lower lip vibrates with each note

SUGGESTIONS

Try out your pizzicato on a Daffy Duck-tiptoe sequence.

Bend your elbows so that your arms are held in close at chest level. Let your wrists go limp. Bend over slightly and produce your pizzicato scale as you stealthily tiptoe your way across the room. You are a perfect Saturday morning cartoon sneak.

THE VIRTUOSO VIOLIN PIZZICATO

THE MANDOLIN

Venice. Naples. Rome. All these can be yours with the mouth mandolin. There is nothing quite like the mandolin to conjure up images of the old country—canals, cappuccino, and overweight people stuffed in Gucci shoes.

The mouth mandolin and a red-checked tablecloth are all you need to set a romantic mood for that certain someone.

INSTRUCTIONS

1. Tuck in your lips and pull them taunt so that your mouth covers your teeth. Do not close your mouth, but keep your lips fairly close together. (If you look in the mirror, you will look like you are doing a pathetic imitation of a toothless, old gondolier.)

2. In your finest falsetto, sing a high, clear tone.

3. While singing the tone, take the tip of your tongue and rapidly brush it up and down across your in-turned lips. This fluttering will break your falsetto tone into the beautifully rapid vibration of a mandolin. (Record)

Your tongue-fluttering may be slow at first, but a little practice will give you the speed needed.

SUGGESTIONS

Try "Santa Lucia" or other such Mediterranean hits on your mouth mandolin. Italians will fight just to stand next to you. The tone of your mandolin will no doubt be improved after a few glasses of Chianti.

THE "SANTA LUCIA" GONDOLIER

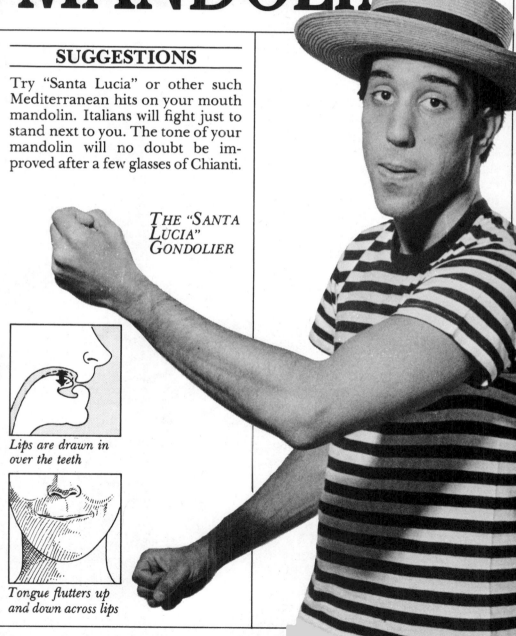

Lips are drawn in over the teeth

Tongue flutters up and down across lips

THE JAZZ BASS

The bass is by far the most sensuous and shapely of musical instruments. Delicate fingered bass players nightly coax out those rich, low moans of the bass in smoky jazz clubs across America. With eyes half closed the bass player strokes, plucks, slaps, bows, or otherwise caresses the bass into groaning its songs.

INSTRUCTIONS

1. With a soft, low tone, sing the sounds "duh, duh, duh."

2. Put your lips together so that your bottom lip protrudes slightly as if you were pouting. Continue saying your low "duh's." The bottom lip should be slightly tensed so that it is blown out a little with the percussion of each "duh." Practice until you get a single, sharp "pluck" of your lip with each note.

3. Work on a musical scale. Keep your "duh's" low, hum-like, and very resonant, just like a bass. As you feel more comfortable with your mouth bass, try plucking your way slowly and sensuously through such songs as "Misty," "Breaking Up Is Hard to Do," "It Had To Be You," or jazz standards such as "Satin Doll." (Record)

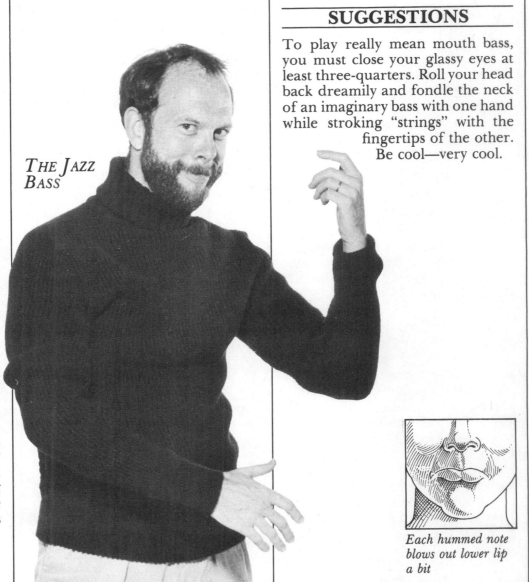

THE JAZZ BASS

SUGGESTIONS

To play really mean mouth bass, you must close your glassy eyes at least three-quarters. Roll your head back dreamily and fondle the neck of an imaginary bass with one hand while stroking "strings" with the fingertips of the other. Be cool—very cool.

Each hummed note blows out lower lip a bit

CLASSICAL GUITAR

The classical guitar is an acoustic guitar played in a concert hall by a long-fingered musician in a black tie. The classical *mouth* guitar, on the other hand, is merely a mouth played by a non-musician, usually while soaking in the bathtub. The sounds and enjoyment are the same. Only the methods and whereabouts differ.

INSTRUCTIONS

1. Follow the instructions for the Violin Pizzicato (page 84). The plucking sound of the lip vibration is similar.

2. In the classical guitar, however, the lip vibration is minimized and the normal or falsetto tone is emphasized to produce a fuller, more robust sound. (Record)

SUGGESTIONS

Try musical scales and then graduate on to any slow, classical music such as Mozart's Minuet in G, Bach's "Air on a G-String," or a stripped-down version of Beethoven's Ninth Symphony. If these are unfamiliar, try "Farmer in the Dell."

PERFORMANCE OF "MINUET IN G"

Lower lip vibrates with each hummed note

ELECTRIC GUITAR

The electric guitar is just a violin with a V-8 engine. To coax the rubbery wails of an electric guitar out of your own mouth, all you have to do is wear tight jeans and imitate a violin. Close your eyes, click your heels together three times, and say "I think I'm Elvis Costello." This creates the proper frame of mind.

INSTRUCTIONS

1. Hold your lips together, but slightly draw in your lower lip to allow your upper teeth to rest on it.

2. Use a high, whining falsetto. Concentrate on projecting the whine up and out through the small opening between your teeth and lower lip. Adjust your lips and mouth until you make a sharp guitar-like tone. (Record)

3. Push air upward from your stomach and diaphragm to produce the wavering swells of a guitar tone by rhythmically varying the pressure. Vibrato in a guitar, as with a violin, is quite important. (Record)

Practice different tones and any favorite guitar riffs until you sound a bit like B. B. King.

New Wave Riffs

SUGGESTIONS

Everyone has at least one friend who is a holdover from the Woodstock generation. Whenever that person hears acid guitar yowls, he will suddenly screw his face into pained expression and instinctively begin fretting an imaginary Fender Telecaster guitar with jerky contortions. This is called "getting into" guitar. You must adopt this body English for your own mouth guitar imitations.

The mouth guitar can be used in combinations with the Bass (page 86) and Drums (page 94) for some fine combo work. Remember to say "man" at the end of each sentence and sprinkle sentences with words like "heavy" and "gig."

Teeth on lower lip sharpen falsetto whine

THE TRUMPET

The trumpet is really a New Year's Eve noisemaker that got out of control. It has more range than paper party horns and certainly looks more professional. Its tones can vary from a slow, silken softness to the grinding "razz" of a strip club.

The trumpet is probably the instrument most to blame for half-time, marching-band versions of "Never on Sunday" and "Climb Every Mountain."

INSTRUCTIONS

1. With a moderately high falsetto, make a single, very nasal tone. To make this tone more nasal-sounding, raise the back of your tongue slightly, as if to say an "a" pronounced in the word "back."

2. Sing the word "taa," as you begin to vocalize each note of a musical scale in your falsetto tone.

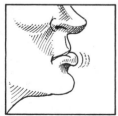

Lower lip vibrates with each note

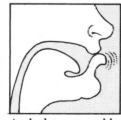

Arched tongue adds nasal quality

Keep thinking of a trumpet sound. Practice your falsetto "taa-taa's" on such trumpet standards as Taps, "Reveille," or a John Philip Sousa march. Throw in a Tijuana Brass and Chuck Mangione number, too.

3. Once you are fairly comfortable with the "taa-taas" and the tone, put your lips together, allowing your bottom lip to protrude slightly with a little tension.

4. Produce your falsetto "taa-taas." Emphasize the "t" of the "taas" so that each "taa" is breathy enough just to blow and vibrate your bottom lip. (Record)

Work at this until you have just the slightest touch of lip vibration with each note. (It may be easier to add this lip vibration from the side of your mouth.)

SUGGESTIONS

Your trumpet provides excellent embellishment to radio music and sounds particularly wonderful solo, in the concert hall of your bathroom. Try your own arrangements of such standards as "Misty," "The Shadow of Your Smile," and "Girl from Ipanema." Delight your friends or fellow office workers by creating your own Muzak in elevators.

Any trumpet player worth a toot, must wear an expression of concentration on his face, using one hand to press imaginary trumpet valves. For those dazzling high notes, be sure to throw your head back, arch your back, and act as if you are in great pain. This gives others the impression you have soul.

THE TRUMPET

THE MUTED TRUMPET

The muted trumpet recalls the bygone era of big bands, fox trots, and huge maroon cars with bulbous fenders. You can create your own brand of nostalgia with the muted mouth trumpet.

INSTRUCTIONS

1. Sing the same nasal "taa-taa's" as you did for the regular mouth trumpet.

2. With the base of the thumb and the third knuckle at the base of the index finger of one hand, gently pinch your nostrils closed. The palm of your hand should cover your mouth and will act as your trumpet mute.

3. As you sing your shrill and nasal "taa-taa's," open and close your cupped hand over your mouth to achieve the "waa-waa" sound of the mute. (Record)

SUGGESTIONS

Practice on a few songs such as "Moonlight Serenade," "You Made Me Love You," and "Auld Lang Syne," but any old tune worth remembering is worth trying. Have several open-minded friends play their muted mouth trumpets and form a veritable big-band era orchestra.

MUTED "MOONLIGHT SERENADE"

THE TROMBONE

The trombone is not, altogether, a particularly versatile instrument. Seldom performed solo before an audience, it is almost always relegated to brassy backup work in large bands.

A metallic blast of a trombone does, however, have the rather special ability to grab a melody and catapult it to the top row of any bleacher. In fact, a good Sunday-afternoon trombone section can deafen and even kill at close range.

Your mouth trombone may not have the raw power of a real thing, but it will have every bit of its flexibility.

INSTRUCTIONS

Follow the directions for the Trumpet (page 89), except that instead of making "taa-taa's" in a high falsetto, produce low-pitched, *deep*, nasal "taa-taa's." The lip vibrations will be identical. (Record)

Lower lip vibrates with each note

SUGGESTIONS

The trombone can be used to play any marching-band classic from John Philip Sousa's "The Stars and Stripes Forever" to "Seventy-six Trombones."

The mouth trombone is a natural for large numbers at a party. Guests can form lines and "razz" their way through marching-band formations in your living room. You might try a halftime favorite such as "A Marching Salute to the American Automobile." Several people form the outline of a car while a few others rotate round-and-round as wheels—all to the tune of "In My Merry Oldsmobile."

"STARS AND STRIPES FOREVER"

THE FRENCH HORN

The French horn is an instrument that has the peculiar quality of sounding as if it is coming from the next room even when it is being played right in front of you. Like a distant sound, the French horn naturally has a muted softness to it. And your imitation of the instrument will reflect this.

INSTRUCTIONS

1. With a moderately high, nasal falsetto, sing the words "boh, boh, boh" in an ascending musical scale. Practice this a few times.

2. Now place your lips together in a relaxed manner.

3. Sing your "bohs," with an especially strong nasal quality. Tense your lips with each note so that your cheeks puff out loosely with the air of each "boh," and then suddenly collapse as the lips vibrate apart and air escapes. You must work toward just a touch of loose lip vibration with each note. (Record)

SUGGESTIONS

You can perfect a near flawless imitation of an English hunting horn with your French horn mouth sound.

A hunting horn makes a fine wake-up call in the ear of a loved one and is guaranteed to rouse even the most comatose sleeper.

Cheeks billow out loosely with each note

THE FRENCH HORN

THE SAXOPHONE

The saxophone or "sax" looks like an instrument right out of a good science-fiction movie. Peppered with all manner of valves and hatches, the saxophone resembles some weird golden space colony.

But the sax is really a very down-to-earth instrument with tremendous range: It can have a mellow fullness unmatched by any other musical instrument, or the gravel-voiced nastiness of the gutter.

The Clean Sax

INSTRUCTION

1. Imitation of the saxophone requires a special hollow resonance of the mouth. Open your mouth partway and draw in your bottom lip tauntly over your bottom teeth.

2. Seal the front edge of your tongue against your bottom lip, arching the back of your tongue up to allow a hollow cavity to form under your tongue. The back of the tongue should almost touch the roof of the mouth.

3. In a normal voice, sing a soft "a" sound. (The "a" should be the sound of the "a" in "back.") Experiment with your lip and arched tongue until you hear a hollow breathy quality to the tone. (Record)

4. Practice a musical scale and work on breath control.

SUGGESTIONS

The mouth sax can be a dead ringer for the real thing. Use vibrato and a sort of throaty breathiness to add realism. Try a soft falsetto, too. This will produce a sound much like the tone of a tenor saxophone. Slow, moody songs like "I've Grown Accustomed to Her Face," "Feelings," "Moon River," and "Yesterday" make perfect dentist office-type sax numbers. With

two friends, one on Brushes and another on the Bass, you can have some dynamite jazz jams.

 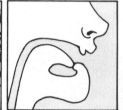

Front edge of tongue seals against tucked lower lip   *Tongue is arched off floor of mouth*

THE DIRTY SAX

Dirty sax is that razzy, jazzy sax with a nasty bite to it. It is the saxophone of 1950s rock 'n' roll.

To make a dirty mouth sax, shape your tongue and mouth as in a normal mouth saxophone, but instead of singing a mellow tone, let your voice explode with a low, harsh "a" (as in "back") sound. The sounds should issue forth with a grunt-like quality. (Record)

The Dirty Sax

THE DRUMS

Drums are the most ancient of musical instruments. No doubt the satisfaction derived from drumming was discovered early in prehistoric times when man first began beating his fellow man.

For your mouth sound repertoire there are four basic percussion effects: the snare drum, the bass drum, the cymbals, and the brushes.

SNARE DRUM

1. Produce the Palate Grind (see page 32).

2. Practice the Palate Grind to make it sound like the rolls of a snare drum. Starting with the back of the tongue raised against the palate, abruptly and explosively make a series of bursting Palate Grinds. (Record)

With the correct rhythm, these Palate Grinds can sound much like the drum cadence of a marching band.

BASS DRUM

After you are accomplished with your snare drum, you can use the Palate Grind to simulate deeper tom-toms and the bass drum.

Close your mouth. Puff out your cheeks slightly with air. As you make a burst of the Palate Grind, simultaneously let your lips explode in a sort of "b" sound. This is the bass drum. Practice this.

If you make this bass drum hammer in a fast-driving beat with a strong "b" sound, you have disco. (Record)

THE DRUM SOLO

CYMBAL

The cymbal is quite easy.

Place your tongue tightly behind your clenched teeth. Allow a sizzling burst of air to abruptly rush past your tongue in a sort of "tssss" sound. (Record)

Practice, letting the hissing sound fade slowly.

Palate Grind produced in the back of the mouth for drums

CIRCUS DRUM ROLL

Produce your snare drum roll, followed immediately by the clash of your mouth cymbal. (Record)

This circus drum roll is a great mouth sound for the inveterate show-off. The roll can be used impressively to add pomp and ceremony to any act from knocking back a beer to tying your shoes. You can hold the rapt attention of an audience during even the most mundane task.

BRUSHES

For jazz buffs, no percussion section would be complete without the smoky sounds of the brushes. Rhythm and softness are important.

In a whispering breath of air, make the sound of "tchi, chu-chu, tchi, chu-chu, tchi" with soft emphasis on the "tchi's." (Record)

Use the brushes in a mouth-sounds jazz combo, with the bass and sax or trumpet. The brushes can be combined in sequence with the snare, bass drum, and cymbal for a real Buddy Rich sound.

HAWAIIAN NOSE HUM

It has been said that the hum is God's gift to those who never remember the words to songs. The Hawaiian Nose Hum represents one of the finest variations of this divine contribution.

INSTRUCTIONS

1. Keep the mouth closed.

2. Press the tip of an index finger beside one nostril, closing it. (*Note:* Do not insert index finger, as you may quickly become the butt of cruel jokes.)

3. With a high falsetto voice, begin humming your favorite Hawaiian melody. Remember to keep your mouth closed. With the free index finger stroke down on the open nostril, closing it momentarily, as you begin each note of the tune. The result should be a mildly percussive, nasal guitar sound. (Record)

Index finger closes open nostril with each note

Develop your own style, using vibrato and hand flourishes to add style and grace. Do not be reticent to nose hum in the bathroom. Tile provides a fine echo effect.

SUGGESTIONS

The Hawaiian Nose Hum can be particularly rewarding when accompanied by a ukulele or in harmonizing choirs of four or more.

THE HAWAIIAN NOSE HUM

Of course, pineapple punch in coconut shells and grass skirts make nice extras.

You can also adopt the basic nose hum to simulate the pedal steel guitar of Country and Western songs. All you have to do is think "Conway Twitty" to draw out those wailing swells of country music. The steel guitar nose hum lends a wonderful touch to late nights at a pancake house or diner, or as an accompanyment to the beer-hall jukebox.

HUMMMMMMMMM.

The word "hum" is a perfect example of a word that is the sound itself. Where did it come from?

The old Dutch word for honeybee was "hommel," a variation of which entered the English language—around the fourteenth century—when the little whirring insect came to be called "humbylebee." Eventually the name changed to the modern "bumblebee," but the root word "hum"—the sound of the bumblebee—stayed with us.

MISCELLANEOUS MOUTHSOUNDS

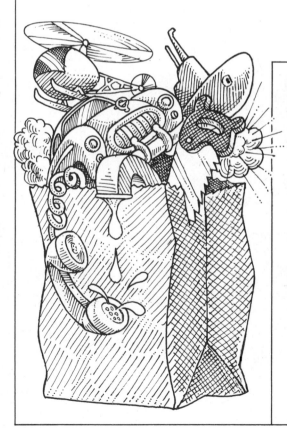

This chapter dips into the soup of sounds that perpetually surrounds us and ladles up servings of some of the most notable. Grouped into bite-sized chunks, the sections—Transportation, Household Noises, and Space Effects—give the reader and would-be-show-off spoonfuls of sounds to be used for storytelling, conversational color, and general attention-getting.

THE DOPPLER EFFECT

TRANSPORTATION

In this age of mobility, we spend great amounts of time sitting quietly, in the dazed state of being conveyed from one spot to another. We may be behind the padded dash of an automobile, on a train or plane staring blankly out the window, or standing on a crowded bus with someone's umbrella in our ribs—but, we are, at least, moving. The sights and sounds of human transportation are an everyday part of our world.

You have just stepped off the curb and are about to cross the street against the light. Suddenly someone in a car speeding toward you sits on the horn—*whaaaa!* You jump back. As the car races past, suddenly the sound of the car horn drops down a note—*whaa-ooo!* In addition to scaring you nearly to death, this little happening demonstrates the Doppler Effect.

Christian Johann Doppler, a nineteenth-century Austrian physicist, first explained this phenomenon. As Doppler described it, sounds from an approaching object are higher pitched to a stationary listener than the same sounds from a receding object. As the sound source approaches, the sound waves become compressed and more vibrations strike the ear per unit of time (causing a sensation that is perceived as higher in pitch). As the sound source moves away, the sound waves effectively become less condensed causing an abrupt lowering of pitch.

In imitating moving objects such as speeding cars, abruptly lower the pitch of the sound to simulate the Doppler Effect.

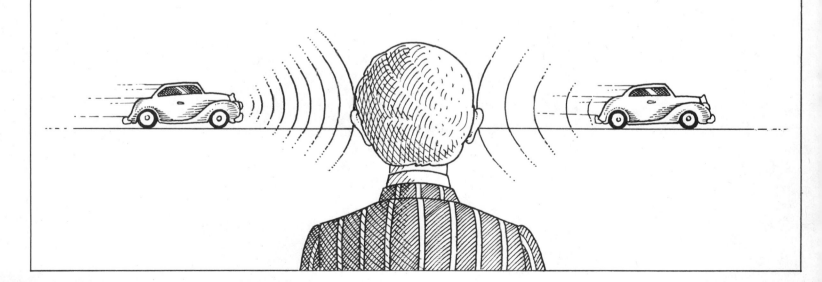

'62 BUICK

Old cars, those huge contraptions with big bumpers, pointy fenders, loads of chrome, and a bent coat hanger for an aerial, plow up and down the avenues and byways of America, spewing out smoke and all sorts of mechanical misfirings.

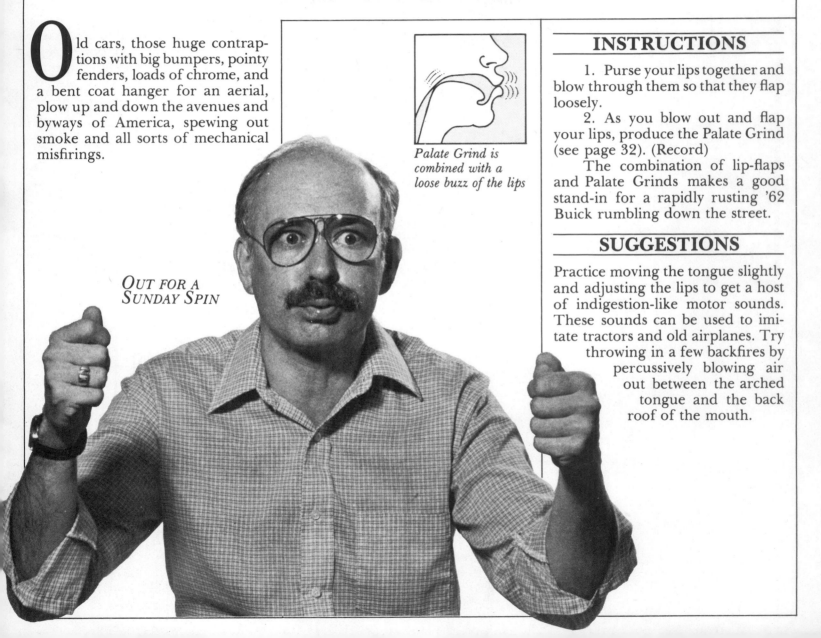

Palate Grind is combined with a loose buzz of the lips

OUT FOR A SUNDAY SPIN

INSTRUCTIONS

1. Purse your lips together and blow through them so that they flap loosely.

2. As you blow out and flap your lips, produce the Palate Grind (see page 32). (Record)

The combination of lip-flaps and Palate Grinds makes a good stand-in for a rapidly rusting '62 Buick rumbling down the street.

SUGGESTIONS

Practice moving the tongue slightly and adjusting the lips to get a host of indigestion-like motor sounds. These sounds can be used to imitate tractors and old airplanes. Try throwing in a few backfires by percussively blowing air out between the arched tongue and the back roof of the mouth.

THE SPORTS CAR

Little red sports cars may be made in Italy, but they are as American as Maxwell House coffee. Their spritely, breezy buzz will quicken the pulse of any sixteen-year-old.

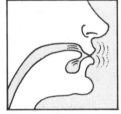

Tongue flutters behind buzzing lips

INSTRUCTIONS

1. This is a two-part sound. To make the first part, push your lips out into a tight pucker, then blow through them to make a moderately high buzzing sound.

2. For the second part, trill your tongue on the front roof of your mouth just as though you were rolling your tongue for a Spanish or Scottish "r."

3. Produce both sounds: the buzz of the pucker and the tongue trill. Experiment until you get this sports car-like sound. (Record)

SUGGESTIONS

Using the Doppler Effect (page 99), imitate the sound of a speeding car by abruptly lowering the pitch of the pucker-buzz as the car passes. (Record) Try simulating the Daytona 500 as cars of different sizes and speeds race past you. (Record)

THE ITALIAN CONVERTIBLE

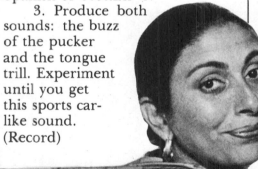

THE HELICOPTER

THE CHOPPER

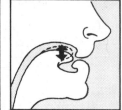

The helicopter is man's version of the bumblebee. Of course, choppers do not make honey or pollinate flowers—but then bees do not bring us on-the-scene radio traffic reports in the morning. It all works out.

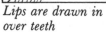

Lips are drawn in over teeth

Tongue flutters up and down across tucked lips

INSTRUCTIONS

1. Draw in your lips tautly so that they cover the upper and lower teeth. (You will look like a toothless old geezer about to down a bowl of oatmeal.)

2. Close your mouth, allowing a small opening between the tucked lips.

3. Draw air in through the opening, as you rapidly run the tip of your tongue up and down across the inward-protruding edges of your lips to produce the "chopping" sound of the helicopter. (Record)

It may take a little time to develop this rapid up and down movement of the tongue (also used for the Mandolin, page 85).

SUGGESTIONS

The helicopter sound can be made gradually louder to similate a landing approach by drawing in greater amounts of air. If made a little breathier, the sound can also be used to imitate birds in flight.

WINGING IT

THE SUBMARINE

Submarines, those underwater cigars, produce a wealth of noises that will make excellent additions to your vocal collection.

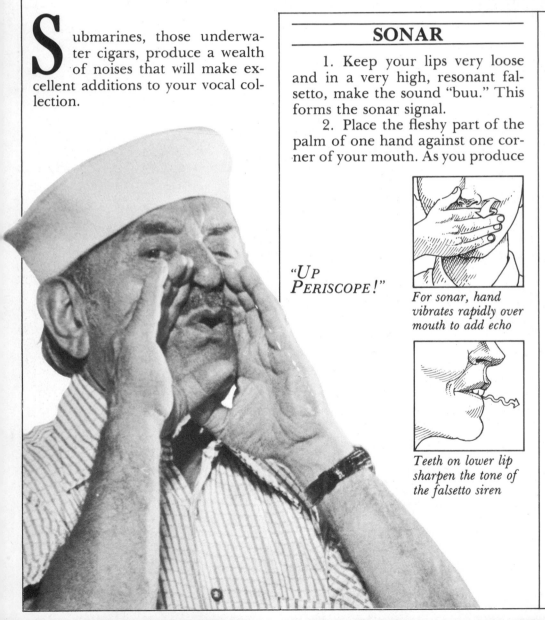

"UP PERISCOPE!"

SONAR

1. Keep your lips very loose and in a very high, resonant falsetto, make the sound "buu." This forms the sonar signal.

2. Place the fleshy part of the palm of one hand against one corner of your mouth. As you produce a series of high-pitched "buu's," rapidly open and close the hand over the mouth so that the sound has an echoey, tremolo effect. (Record)

You now have the background sound for your own version of the movie *Up Periscope*.

For sonar, hand vibrates rapidly over mouth to add echo

Teeth on lower lip sharpen the tone of the falsetto siren

THE DIVE

The following sounds are done in rapid sequence.

1. **The Siren:** Put your lips nearly together. Draw in your lower lip slightly so that your upper teeth rest on your lower lip. (As the siren issues forth from your throat, the teeth and lips will muffle it a bit.)

2. In your most nasal falsetto, hum a loud tone. Let it rise and fall rythmically in pitch as a siren does. Practice until you maintain sufficient volume and control. (Record)

3. **The "Ah-ooo-gah":** The siren is followed by a guttural "aaa-oooooo-gah," created in a gravelly fashion at the back of your throat. (Record)

4. Cup your hands over your mouth to muffle your voice so it sounds like it's coming over a loudspeaker and say in a low-pitched, nasal voice, "Dive, dive . . ."

THE WATER DRIP

HOUSEHOLD SOUNDS

The household is a veritable treasure trove of noises. The blender whirring, the backdoor slamming, the bacon sizzling, the telephone ringing all combine to form a domestic symphony.

Drip. Drip. Drip. Drip. Who has not, at one time or another, buried their head in a pillow in anguish, trying to blot out the persistent "ploit" of a leaky tap? Drip. Drip. Drip. There is something so penetrating, so perplexing about the delicate "plop" of dripping water.

INSTRUCTIONS

1. Close off the back of your mouth by breathing normally through your nose. Draw your tongue to the back of your mouth. Shape your lips into a whistle-pucker, with an approximately ⅛-inch round hole in the center of your lips.

2. Push your tongue forward rapidly in such a way that you force a little burst of air through your puckered lips to produce a slight whistle. (Record)

Practice this until you get a little whistle tone that is produced solely by the action of your tongue pushing air forward. (Do *not* whistle by blowing out air from your lungs, as in a normal whistle).

3. After mastering this whistle effect, thump lightly on the hollow of your cheek to create a single "Ploit" (see Ploit Principle, page 31). Your tongue should be well back and your lips in a whistle-pucker. Just as you thump on your cheek, push the tongue forward to make the whistle. *Drip!* (Record)

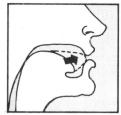

Tongue pushes forward with lips puckered to produce a whistle . . .

. . . and a well-timed thump on the cheek makes the drip

THE WATER DRIP, DRIP, DRIP

SUGGESTIONS

Because the Water Drip is so realistic, use it completely out of context in the classroom, dentist's waiting room, at dinner, or over cocktails to impress and/or confuse acquaintances. The Water Drip becomes impressive, indeed, when amplified by microphone or telephone.

THE BLOW DRYER

Hair dryers were once huge helmet contraptions found hovering over the heads of women reading magazines in beauty parlors. No longer relegated to the tint-and-rinse set, hair dryers have invaded the bathrooms of America. Every morning at 7:15 sharp, millions of wet-haired Americans bravely subject themselves to the seering, whirring, and whining of a 1,000-watt pistol-grip.

THE 1,000-WATT HAIR DRYER

INSTRUCTIONS

1. To make the sound of a hair dryer you first of all have to master the Fingerless Whistle (page 77). Follow the directions for the whistle, but blow gently, making a fairly low-pitched, soft whistle.

2. As you whistle, hum a long, low note. The combination of the low whistle and the hum makes a very realistic blow dryer imitation. (Record)

SUGGESTIONS

Use the Blow Dryer to bamboozle others. In front of a mirror at a posh party, for instance, go through the motions of blow-drying while producing the sound. Or as a conversation starter, blow-dry the locks of an attractive someone. If you happen to be bored in a department store, walk over to the hair dryer display, pick up a sample, and proceed to style your hair with the unplugged dryer. The salesclerk will be speechless.

The blow dryer effect can also be used to imitate a wide range of other whirring gadgets from Vacuum cleaners to blenders.

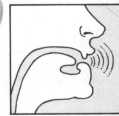

As in the Fingerless Whistle, tongue is arched off floor of mouth

Produce the Taxi Whistle and hum at the same time

THE TELEPHONE DIAL

Rotary dialing on our telephones will soon be a thing of the past. Like many old-fashioned clicks and whirrs, the dialing of the phone is rapidly being replaced by the "beeps" and "blips" of electronic push buttons. At least vocally, we must preserve the classic sound of the phone dial.

INSTRUCTIONS

1. With lips slightly open, clench teeth together.

2. Withdraw the tongue to the back of the mouth.

3. Now blow out sharply through your teeth to make a hissing sound. As you make this hiss, forcefully ram the tongue forward to seal it against the back of the teeth, abruptly halting the hiss.

4. With the tongue fully forward, quickly follow the hiss with a series of clicking sounds. Create these little sucking sounds between the tongue and front roof of your mouth. Each rushing hiss is followed by varying numbers of clicking sounds. (Record)

SUGGESTIONS

Make a loose fist, then extend your thumb and your baby finger only. Place the thumb near your ear and the extended pinky finger near your mouth, for a makeshift phone receiver. With the other hand, dial the imaginary phone.

Blow through clenched teeth for a hiss and thrust tongue forward . . .

. . . followed by a quick series of clicks made with sucking motions of tongue

THE TELEPHONE DIAL

THE SAW

The sound of the suburban hand saw is a sign of a real do-it-yourselfer—the kind of do-it-yourselfer who can actually construct rickety bookshelves. Never mind if they lean to one side and can only support four books, it is the recreation of hammering and sawing that is important.

INSTRUCTIONS

1. Produce a rhythmic series of Palate Grinds (see page 32).

2. To make the downward-rasp of the saw, combine a falsetto tone that glides up in pitch with each Palate Grind.

3. Between each thrust of the Palate Grind and falsetto, inhale through clenched teeth to make the sawing sound. (Record).

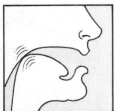

Along with falsetto whine, Palate Grinds are produced in back of mouth

THE HAND SAW AT WORK

SUGGESTIONS

Of course, no saw sound is complete without a back and forth sawing motion of your arm. Using only an ordinary knife and fork, use the saw imitation at a meal to hint that, perhaps, the steak is tough. Or inflict psychological damage on your spouse, kid brother, or classmate by "sawing" through various sections of their midriff and limbs. At your next party, you might try sawing a lady in half.

HUM AND WHISTLE MULTIPURPOSE SPACE EFFECT

SPACE EFFECTS

In the futuristic frontiers of space, sounds take on the form of exotic "swooshes," fantastic "bleeps," and echoing bangs—at least that is the way Hollywood tells it. And who is to argue? Few of us have chanced our way to the Andromeda galaxy.

In reality, closing a door in a space colony may sound exactly like slamming a screen door in Skokie, Illinois. But that *is* unimaginative. The wonder of space effects is that they may sound as outrageous and unbelievable as you want.

The Hum and Whistle Multipurpose Space Effect is just the thing for zapping your way through steel doors, beaming around protoplasm, and generally phasing your friends out of exist-ence. It can form the sound of hovering starships and intergalactic communicators. For those of you in need of a death ray, the hum and whistle should fill the bill nicely.

DEFENDING THE GALAXY

INSTRUCTIONS:

1. Follow the instructions for the Pucker Whistle (page 72).

2. As you produce the Pucker Whistle, hum a low steady note. (Record)

SUGGESTIONS

Once you have perfected the hum and whistle, raise and lower the pitch of the whistle while keeping the hum constant. This lends an eerie Hollywood-type realism to the sound.

Snuggle up close to the ear of a dozing friend and lovingly jolt them with the hum and whistle stun ray. For a couple of days, they may treat you like an alien.

THE LASER GUN

The laser gun will be a favorite of anyone who secretly yearns to be Luke Skywalker. It forms a fine defense against such cosmic scourges as demon extra-terrestrials, enemy star fleets, and cosmic insurance agents.

LASERING AN ENEMY ALIEN

INSTRUCTIONS

1. Say the word "cue." Notice that the tongue touches the roof of the mouth.

2. Repeat the word very slowly, but this time do not finish the word. Keep the tongue on the roof of the mouth and continue to let air rush past. With a sort of rolling motion, slide the tongue back along the roof of your mouth and you will get a rushing "swoosh" of a sound. (Record)

Practice until you have what you imagine as the electronic burst of a laser.

SUGGESTIONS

Once you have mastered the Laser Gun, try beginning each "swoosh" by forming your mouth as if you were saying a "th" sound. Start with a "th" and, with a rapid, fluid motion, slide the tongue back to form the "cue" sound. This will give your Laser Gun added punch.

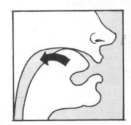

Arch of tongue rolls back on roof of mouth for "swoosh" sound

INTERGALACTIC GISMO

ROBOT WHIRRS

Basically, all space machines sound alike. They make a sort of humming, whirring sound that satisfies even the most hardened science-fiction buffs. The Intergalactic Gismo is a general-purpose whirrr that can be used to imitate an interplanetary assortment of machines, such as space-ships, robots, control boards, and air-lock doors.

INSTRUCTIONS

1. Make the sound of the letter "j."

2. As you make the "j" sound, hum a low-pitched tone to draw out the "j" into a sort of mechanical whirr. (Record)

SUGGESTIONS

You can perform a pretty good rendition of a robot by slowly and stiffly moving your appendages about to the sound of your gismo whirr. At the end of each motion, terminate the sound with a sharp "ch" sound. Use your robot to disrupt gatherings and cooly molest others.

RUDE NOISES

Rudeness, as an existential concept, is a satisfying indifference to what is generally accepted to be "good form." It can range from the inelegant to the offensive, from discourteous to indecent. Rudeness can be tasteless, uncivilized, insolent, or just shamelessly malodorous.

But rudeness is not an act. It is a state of mind, an attitude. Rudeness exists in its own right—in the intent of the initiator. The implication here is that even if we are absolutely alone, we can still officially be disgusting. This is a comforting thought. A belch alone at midnight is just as pleasurably rude as a belch in Tiffany's.

Quite often we would like to tell a

certain someone to go suck an egg, but our upbringing, the pressures of society, and general decorum restrain us. Because our vocabulary is limited, we may be forced to deny ourselves the pleasure of displaying our rudeness to others.

The purpose, then, of this chapter is to help you expand your vocabularly from traditional words and actions into the ever-so-subtle realm of crude and offensive noises. By incorporating these noises into your own rubrics of rudeness, you can better exercise and satisfy the more barbaric undercurrents of your psyche.

THE RASPBERRY

BODY SOUNDS

Let's get down to basics. Body sounds are a part of life. Although we may try to cover them up, push them down or deny them, they are with us every step.

Body sounds are an inescapable part of the life process. Our best strategy is not to treat them as ugly stepchildren, but embrace them wholeheartedly and bring them into our service.

The Raspberry or Bronx Cheer is the granddaddy of body sounds. From the time Roman senators first used them to pooh-pooh fellow senators, Raspberries have been a part of our society. Chaucer, Shakespeare, and Faulkner are just a few of the literary giants whose characters wheel and deal in raspberries.

Psychologically, the Raspberry is the poor man's protest. Even a person in the most powerless position can, at least, give authority a good "razz."

The Raspberry is legal. It makes a point and, if nothing else, is therapeutic.

INSTRUCTIONS

1. Close your mouth, protrude your tongue through your lips, and then force out air. "Razzz." What a fine sound, full of history and tradition. (Record)

2. Complement the basic Raspberry by placing the thumb of your opened hand against your nose and waggling the fingers to add a little more insult.

THE CLASSIC RASPBERRY (WITH HAND FLOURISH)

SUGGESTIONS

The Raspberry (with hand flourish) is perfect behind the back of authority figures—parents, teachers, business superiors, flight attendants, and Congressmen. Particularly if done with their backs turned, authorities are none the wiser, and you score points with your colleagues for launching at least a modest protest.

Be creative. Use the Raspberry to signal a slow waiter for the check, wave good-bye to a mother-in-law, or provocatively signal a good-looker in a singles bar.

THE FIZZLE RAZZ

THE FIZZLE RAZZ, CON BRIO

Teeth over lower lip, blow out side of mouth

The Fizzle Razz does not have the rich tradition of the Raspberry, but it is certainly nastier and more offensive.

INSTRUCTIONS

1. Pull your lower lip into your mouth and place your upper teeth firmly over it.

2. Force air out through one corner of your mouth to produce a particularly deep and ugly razz with your upper lip. (Record)

Experiment with varying lip tensions and air pressure to develop your own distinct, rude, spluttering sound.

SUGGESTIONS

The Fizzle Razz is a direct affront, delivered as a face-to-face assault. It can be used in a heated argument in place of a verbal insult. But do be discreet in wielding the Fizzle Razz. You can wind up having your lips ripped off.

EROTIC RASPBERRY

The Erotic Raspberry is the most social of all raspberries, for it takes a team of two to pull it off—a razzer and a razzee. After proper introduction, the razzer gently requests permission to expose the stomach of the razzee. When given the nod, the razzer lifts up the shirt or blouse of the razzee, places his or her mouth on the soft belly, and then blows out forcefully. *Razzzz!* (Record)

SUGGESTIONS

The Erotic Raspberry takes on a liquid quality if produced in the shower, and a greasy, sliding quality if attempted at surf-side with the aid of suntan lotion. Public attempts of the Erotic Raspberry are discouraged, however. They might get you jailed on moral charges.

The Razzer

The Razzee

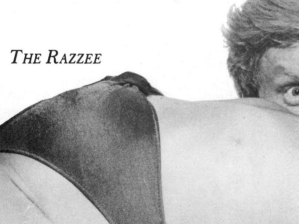

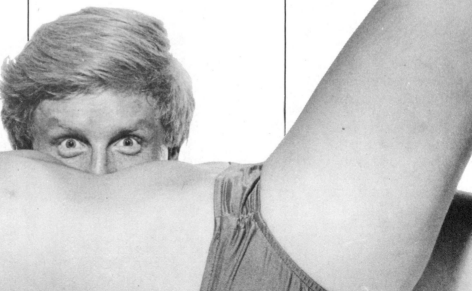

THE ERSATZ BURP

Burps, those guttural fireworks, are always lurking somewhere in the depths of our throats. The fuse is lit with 16-ounce soft drinks, sausage pizza, Rice-a-Roni, shrimp creole, or fast-food tacos. Then, suddenly, when we least expect it—*burrrrrrp!* We may try to swallow it, stifle it, or run for cover, but despite all efforts it explodes in all its wonder.

But the burp is our friend. In some cultures a resounding burp is a sign of gastronomic enjoyment, in others it can get you taken off the invitation list. The burp is the archenemy of the overly polite, up-tight matron who wears hats and sips tea with the pinkie extended.

We should be proud of the burp. It is, at least, an audible affirmation that we are alive and digesting.

The Ersatz Burp is a refined simulation of the real burp. It is quite unlike the emanations from those grammar school cutups who gulp down bushels of air and then belch loudly upon command. That is a finely honed skill to be sure, but it does not have the controlled elegance of the Ersatz Burp.

INSTRUCTIONS

1. Practice the Inhaled Glottal Fry (page 40). Open your throat as wide as possible and produce as deep an Inhaled Glottal Fry as you can.

2. Try bursting out in a low "errr" sound. Then try articulating the sound "breep." (Record)

THE ERSATZ BURP

With a little work you can develop a resonate, artificial burp that has your personality.

SUGGESTIONS

Picture yourself on a plane or bus sitting next to a talkative woman with body odor. The situation is clearly unbearable, but you have the window seat and do not want to move. Solution? The Ersatz Burp.

As the woman jabbers on about her childhood in Milwaukee and the latest illness of a pet, burp. That will stop conversation momentarily. Fake an apology, then burp again. Act disturbed, and mention motion sickness. Lean toward her.

The woman will quietly excuse herself and you can then sleep, gaze out the window, or read in privacy.

The Ersatz Burp is just the thing whenever a bit of anarchy is needed. It is a must for an overly intense chemistry class and just the thing for loosening up a luncheon date.

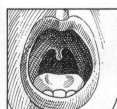

Mouth open wide to add resonance and quality

STOMACH GROWLS

Stomach growls are cosmic. They are those little whirr-and-whistle messages from the inner sanctum of our digestive tract. They are cryptic communications from the galaxy of plumbing within us. Stomach growls are uncontrollable, unpredictable, and, in a quiet room, undeniable. But, they are always funny.

INSTRUCTIONS

Practice the Inhaled Glottal Fry until you articulate a very soft low "o-ree, o-ree" sound that varies in pitch. Keep your mouth almost closed. (Record)

SUGGESTIONS

Just like real stomach growls, your simulations should be low and subtle and reserved for intimate, quiet moments. If you suddenly get to an awkward topic of conversation, use the Stomach Growl to create a temporary diversion. Act good-naturedly surprised, apologize profusely and quickly change the subject. The effect can be a life saver during a sticky discussion at business lunches and in delicate social situations.

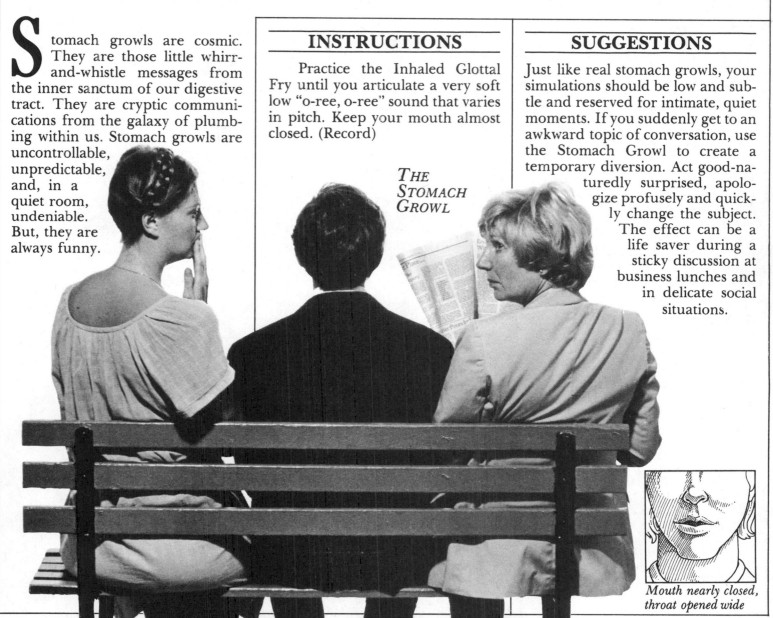

THE STOMACH GROWL

Mouth nearly closed, throat opened wide

THE NOSE BLOW

One of those little rituals of the winter season is blowing the nose. In the past, we would wait for a private moment, extract a neatly folded handkerchief, unfold it methodically, place it over our nose, and blow discreetly into its monogrammed folds. But times have changed.

Now, whenever we get the urge, we yank out a crumpled Kleenex, slap it to our face, and let it rip. Genteel nasal clearing may be a thing of the past. But so much the better. This gives you added creative possibilities in using your artificial Nose Blow.

INSTRUCTIONS

1. Keeping the front of your tongue on the floor of your mouth, arch the middle of your tongue upward to touch the roof of your slightly opened mouth.

2. Blow out air so that it flows *under* the tongue. You should get a gravelly, "razzing" sound as the bottom of the tongue vibrates against the floor of your mouth. Experiment with this.

3. Cup your hands over your mouth and nose, and produce your under-the-tongue "razz." It will sound very much like a good, strong blowing of your nose. (Record)

SUGGESTIONS

You can use the Nose Blow for a gag, equalled in effect only by the plastic vomit and spring-loaded chewing gum tricks. Spying your victim, compliment him on his tie and lift it up admiringly for a closer

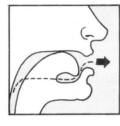

Blow air under tongue for nose-blowing sound

look. Press it to your face and simulate your robust nose blow. What a fine way to set the tone for an office Christmas party.

To be the hit of your neighbor's next anniversary party, "blow your nose" on their new living room curtains.

THE ARTIFICIAl NOSE BLOW

LABORED BREATHING

Labored Breathing, if nothing else, is the rallying cry for millions of obscene phone callers around the world. Through years of field research and experience, the League of Obscene Phone Callers (LOPC) has found Labored Breathing to induce more female hysteria than any other disgusting body sound.

INSTRUCTIONS

1. With eyes half closed, let your tongue rest on the bottom lip of your opened mouth. Bend over a little and leer if possible.

2. Make a very low, groaning "aah" sound and breathe heavily, both in and out. This is Labored Breathing. (Record)

If you are thinking filthy thoughts, you are probably breaking the law.

SUGGESTIONS

Labored Breathing is now considered unfashionable by trend-setters in the field of public nuisance. Not only does it lack style and originality, but its sheer effectiveness renders it unsportsman-like as well.

Labored Breathing can be used harmlessly, however, while listening to recorded weather forecasts or movie times over the phone, or in response to telephone solicitations.

"AH-AAGH-AAH-HAAH"

ELEVATOR LABORED BREATHING

Elevators are an anomaly in our world. For a few seconds, we are locked into a tiny room with total strangers. What better time to take advantage of your fellow man than that unique moment of vulnerability.

With an accomplice, walk into a crowded elevator. Stoop a bit and produce your best Labored Breathing. Your friend should stand beside you with his or her mouth and nose covered with a handkerchief. Through the muffle of the protective cloth, the accomplice asks in voice loud enough for all to hear: "Just what exactly did the doctor say you had?" As you continue to breathe loudly, all other breathing on the elevator will stop. When the doors next open, there is usually a mass exodus or, at the very least, a group of elevator riders with bulging eyes and cheeks and a bluish tinge to their faces.

THE SPLAT

GENERALLY DISGUSTING SOUNDS

In the vast sea of sound around us, there are some distinctive noises that noticeably bob to the surface—those particular sounds that are unsavory, disgusting, or otherwise repulsive. These sounds range from suggestive to unpleasantly abstract. They have the ability to conjure up images of pillowy, gooey things and nasty situations.

Because generally disgusting sounds have such emotional presence, they make excellent additions to your vocal menagerie.

The Splat is used by nature to indicate the moment of impact of any gelatinous blob. It is the sound of custard pie in the face, meat loaf dropped from waist level, or wet flounder thrown against the wall. Clearly, the Splat qualifies for inclusion in the Disgusting Sound Hall of Fame.

INSTRUCTIONS

1. Draw your tongue back into your mouth as far as possible.
2. Tense your lips into a slight pucker. Blow air through them in such a way that they vibrate to produce a moderate "buzz."
3. As you make the "buzz," ram your tongue forward to reduce the cavity within your mouth. Push your tongue quickly all the way forward and out between your buzzing lips to create the Splat effect. (Record)

Splats can be long and disgustingly drawn out or short and quick. Try variations.

SUGGESTIONS

The Splat is a fine, general-purpose effect that should be slipped into conversation during appropriate (or for that matter, inappropriate) moments.

THE SPLAT

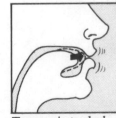

Tongue is pushed forward through buzzing lips

CHEEK MUSIC

Cheek Music is a juicy, abstract sound that is downright filthy. It does not simulate any one sound in particular, but rather suggests a whole host of offensive goings-on.

INSTRUCTIONS

1. Relax your face completely with your mouth closed loosely.

2. Pinch your cheek lightly with the thumb and crook of the index finger.

3. Pull out and push in the relaxed cheek very rapidly. You will get a repulsive, liquid and slurpy sound. (Record)

SUGGESTIONS

If you are fortunate enough to have large jowls, your Cheek Music can be even more rude. (Imagine the Cheek Music Richard Nixon could make, for instance.)

Double the indignity by making Cheek Music on both cheeks for a sort of slushy stereo effect.

Cheek pinched and moved rapidly back and forth

DOUBLE
CHEEK
MUSIC

THE BUBBLE EFFECT

The Bubble Effect is for sheer surprise and sounds rudely suggestive.

INSTRUCTIONS

1. Close off the back of your mouth by breathing normally through your nose. Poke out your bottom lip.

2. Take the finger of one hand and let it flip down on the lower lip to make the lip snap back against the upper lip with a popping sound. Widen the back of your mouth and move your tongue forward and backward to maximize the pop and change its tone.

3. Once you feel comfortable with your single lip-pop, use the four fingertips of one hand to snap your bottom lip. Rotate your fingers down across your lip in sequence, starting with the tip of the little finger and rolling fluidly to the tip of the index finger. You should get a sequence of four quick bubble-like pops.

4. Now do the same sequence of pops with your other hand. By quickly alternating hands, you can get a continuous sequence of bubbley pops. (Record)

SUGGESTIONS

Add zest to your effervescent bubbles by shifting your tongue back and forth in your mouth, simultaneously lowering and raising the floor of your mouth. (Do not move your jaw, only the muscles on the floor of your mouth and throat.)

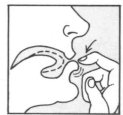
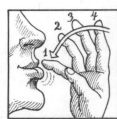

Back of mouth closed, finger snaps lips *Sequence of fingers produces bubbling sound*

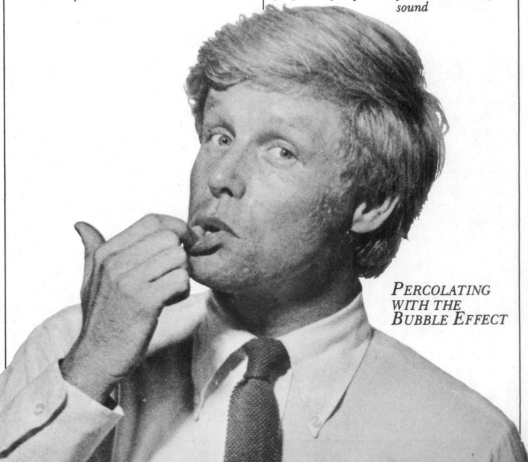

PERCOLATING WITH THE BUBBLE EFFECT

THE BOING

The Boing is a sound popularized by Saturday morning cartoons. It is the reverberating wallop of a frying pan on the head, a coyote leaping with bed spring shoes, and the sudden rake-in-the-face from a wisecracking rooster's careless step. The Boing is not a natural sound we encounter in our daily lives. It is the product of the cartoon animator's fertile imagination.

INSTRUCTIONS

The mouth Boing is produced by pronouncing the word "boing" in a deep, exaggerated fashion.

1. Make the vibrating quality of the "boing" by saying "Boy-oi-oi-ng" in a drawn-out manner. Create the "oi's" by rapidly pushing the tongue slightly forward and backward in your mouth. It may take practice to develop the proper speed of your "oi's."

2. Cup your hands over your mouth and nose as you say your "boy-oi-oi-ng," and rapidly open and close the cup, by shaking one hand from the hinge of your wrist. This hand action gives added echo to your Boing. (Record).

Open and close cupped hands to add echo

Tongue moves back and forth rapidly

SUGGESTIONS

Use the Boing to spruce up your conversational chatter. When you have a bright idea, preface it with a "boing." Try answering the phone with a Boing instead of the traditional "hello." For those callers who do not hang up, the Boing is appreciated as a frank revelation of your mental state.

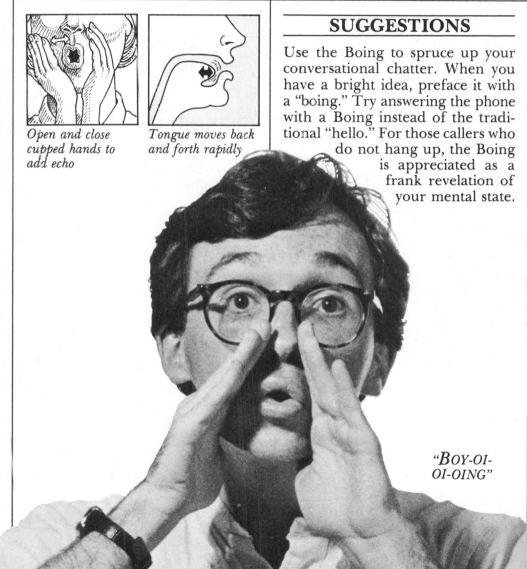

"BOY-OI-OI-OING"

THE SMOCK

The smock is a sound rooted squarely in the abstract expressionist school of mouth sounds. It represents no particular sound from life, but is rather a fanciful flight into the world of crude sounds.

INSTRUCTIONS

1. Seal your lips together.
2. Abruptly pull them apart by opening your mouth while sucking in air. The effect is a single motion, much like a gigantic "smack." (Record)

SUGGESTIONS

The Smock resembles the sound of a plumber's friend on a baby's stomach or, oddly enough, someone walking in wooden clogs. You can use the smock in repetition as a general-purpose noise to irritate family, teachers, or co-workers.

THE SMOCK

Sealed together, lips are sucked into the mouth . . .

. . . and the mouth is abruptly opened

THE MUD TRUDGE

Kids adore it; Mothers abhor it—mud tracks through the life of each and every one of us. Some of us yearn for that magic day in spring when the first warm mud oozes up between our toes. Six-year-olds play patty-cake in it. The ultra-chic use it for facials.

Most of the time mud lies quietly, but when we get a chance to walk through it, it sucks at our heels with its slurpy, guttural voice. The Mud Trudge is a rich, raw sound that will serve you well.

INSTRUCTIONS

1. Place your flattened tongue on the roof of your mouth loosely.
2. As you slowly open your mouth, draw in air so that your inner cheeks vibrate against the side edge of your tongue. Fully open your mouth so that you pull your tongue from the roof of your mouth. (Record)

Practice this (in privacy), working toward a smooth, easy motion that produces the gooey sound of mud.

SUGGESTIONS

Your Mud Trudge can be used to simulate the sound of dog food glopping out of a can or the sound of a plumber's friend in action. With the Mud Trudge you can add a colorful sound effect to the serving of mashed potatoes at your next family gathering.

Back of tongue drawn from roof of mouth as air passes around sides

THE MUD TRUDGE